PRAISE FOR *DEBATING AMERICAN HISTORY*

"*Debating American History* repositions the discipline of history as one that is rooted in discovery, investigation, and interpretation."
—Ingrid Dineen-Wimberly,
University of California, Santa Barbara

"*Debating American History* is an excellent replacement for a 'big assignment' in a course. Offering a way to add discussion to a class, it is also a perfect 'active learning' assignment, in a convenient package."
—Gene Rhea Tucker, Temple College

"The advantage that *Debating American History* has over other projects and texts currently available is that it brings a very clear and focused organization to the notion of classroom debate. The terms of each debate are clear. The books introduce students to historiography and primary sources. Most of all, the project re-envisions the way that US history should be taught. No other textbook or set of teaching materials does what these books do when taken together as the sum of their parts."
—Ian Hartman, University of Alaska

DEBATING AMERICAN HISTORY

INDUSTRIALIZATION AND SOCIAL CONFLICT IN THE GILDED AGE

DEBATING AMERICAN HISTORY

Series Editors: Joel M. Sipress, David J. Voelker

Conflict and Accommodation in Colonial New Mexico

The Powhatans and the English in the Seventeenth-Century Chesapeake

Democracy and the US Constitution

The Causes of the Civil War

Emancipation and the End of Slavery

Industrialization and Social Conflict in the Gilded Age

DEBATING AMERICAN HISTORY

INDUSTRIALIZATION AND SOCIAL CONFLICT IN THE GILDED AGE

Joel M. Sipress

UNIVERSITY OF WISCONSIN–SUPERIOR

NEW YORK   OXFORD
OXFORD UNIVERSITY PRESS

Oxford University Press is a department of the University of Oxford.
It furthers the University's objective of excellence in research, scholarship,
and education by publishing worldwide. Oxford is a registered trade mark of
Oxford University Press in the UK and certain other countries.

Published in the United States of America by Oxford University Press
198 Madison Avenue, New York, NY 10016, United States of America.

For titles covered by Section 112 of the US Higher Education
Opportunity Act, please visit www.oup.com/us/he for the latest
information about pricing and alternate formats.

Library of Congress Cataloging-in-Publication Data

Names: Sipress, Joel M., author.
Title: Industrialization and social conflict in the Gilded Age / Joel M.
    Sipress
Description: New York : Oxford University Press, 2019. | Series: Debating
    American history | Includes bibliographical references and index.
Identifiers: LCCN 2018059884| ISBN 9780190057060 (pbk.) | ISBN 9780190057190
    (ebook)
Subjects: LCSH: Industrialization—Social aspects—United
    States—History—19th century. | Social conflict—United
    States—History—19th century. | United States—Social
    conditions—1865–1918. | United States—Economic conditions—1865–1918.
Classification: LCC E168 .S595 2019 | DDC 973.8—dc23 LC record available at
    https://lccn.loc.gov/2018059884

Printing number: 9 8 7 6 5 4 3 2 1
Printed by LSC Communications, Inc., United States of America

TABLE OF CONTENTS

LIST OF FIGURES

ABOUT THE AUTHOR

Joel M. Sipress received his PhD in United States history from the University of North Carolina at Chapel Hill. He is a Professor of History at the University of Wisconsin-Superior, where he teaches US and Latin American History. He has published articles and book chapters on the history of the US South with a focus on the role of race and class in late nineteenth-century southern politics. He has also written essays on teaching and learning history, including "Why Students Don't Get Evidence and What We Can Do About It," *The History Teacher* 37 (May 2004): 351–363; and "The End of the History Survey Course: The Rise and Fall of the Coverage Model," coauthored with David J. Voelker, *Journal of American History* 97 (March 2011): 1050–1066, which won the 2012 Maryellen Weimer Scholarly Work on Teaching and Learning Award. He serves as co-editor of *Debating American History* with David J. Voelker.

ACKNOWLEDGMENTS

We owe gratitude to Aeron Haynie, Regan Gurung, and Nancy Chick for introducing us and pairing us to work on the Signature Pedagogies project many years ago, as well as to the UW System's Office of Professional and Instructional Development (OPID), which supported that endeavor. Brian Wheel, formerly with Oxford University Press, helped us develop the idea for *Debating American History* and started the project rolling. We want to thank Charles Cavaliere at Oxford for taking on the project and seeing it through to publication, and Anna Russell for her excellent production work. Joel thanks the University of Wisconsin–Superior for support from a sabbatical, and David thanks the University of Wisconsin–Green Bay for support from a Research Scholar grant. David would also like to thank his colleagues in humanities, history, and First Nations Studies, who have been supportive of this project for many years, and Joel thanks his colleagues in the Department of Social Inquiry. We are also indebted to our colleagues (too numerous to mention) who have advanced the Scholarship of Teaching and Learning within the field of history. Without their efforts, this project would not have been possible. We would also like to thank the reviewers of this edition: Linda Tomlinson, Fayetteville State University; John D. Fairfield, Xavier University; Shauna Hann, United States Military Academy; Michael Holm, Boston University; Raymond J. Krohn, Boise State University; Joseph Locke, University of Houston-Victoria; Ted Moore, Salt Lake Community College; Andrew L. Slap, East Tennessee State University; Philip Levy, University of South Florida; Ingrid Dineen-Wimberly, U of Calif., Santa Barbara and U of La Verne; Kristin Hargrove, Grossmont College; Melanie Beals Goan, University of Kentucky; Paul Hart, Texas State University; Ross A. Kennedy, Illinois State University; Scott Laderman, University of Minnesota, Duluth; John Putnam, San Diego State University; and, Matt Tribbe, University of Houston.

SERIES INTRODUCTION

Although history instruction has grown richer and more varied over the past few decades, many college-level history teachers remain wedded to the coverage model, whose overriding design principle is to cover huge swaths of history, largely through the use of textbooks and lectures. The implied rationale supporting the coverage model is that students must be exposed to a wide array of facts, narratives, and concepts to have the necessary background both to be effective citizens and to study history at a more advanced level—something that few students actually undertake. Although coverage-based courses often afford the opportunity for students to encounter primary sources, the imperative to cover an expansive body of material dominates these courses; and the main assessment technique, whether implemented through objective or written exams, is to require students to identify or reproduce authorized knowledge.

Unfortunately, the coverage model has been falling short of its own goals since its very inception in the late nineteenth century. Educators and policymakers have been lamenting the historical ignorance of American youth going back to at least 1917, as Stanford professor of education Sam Wineburg documented in his illuminating exposé of the history of standardized tests of historical knowledge.[1] In 2010, the *New York Times* declared that "History is American students' worst subject," basing this judgment on yet another round of abysmal standardized test scores.[2] As we have documented in our own historical research, college professors over the past century have episodically criticized the coverage model and offered alternatives. Recently, however, college-level history instructors have been forming a scholarly community to improve the teaching of the introductory course by doing research that includes rigorous analysis of student learning. A number of historians who have become involved in this discipline-based pedagogical research,

---

1   Sam Wineburg, "Crazy for History," *Journal of American History* 90 (March 2004): 1401–1414.
2   Sam Dillon, "U.S. Students Remain Poor at History, Tests Show," *New York Times*, June 14, 2011. Accessed online at http://www.nytimes.com/2011/06/15/education/15history.html?emc=eta1&pagewanted=print.

known as the Scholarship of Teaching and Learning (SoTL), have begun to mount a challenge to the coverage model.[3]

Not only has the coverage model often achieved disappointing results by its own standards, it also proves ineffective at helping students learn how to think historically, which has long been a stated goal of history education. As Lendol Calder argued in a seminal 2006 article, the coverage model works to "cover up" or "conceal" the nature of historical thinking.[4] The eloquent lecture or the unified textbook narrative reinforces the idea that historical knowledge consists of a relatively straightforward description of the past. Typical methods of covering content hide from students not only the process of historical research—the discovery and interpretation of sources—but also the ongoing and evolving discussions among historians about historical meaning. In short, the coverage model impedes historical thinking by obscuring the fact that history is a complex, interpretative, and argumentative discourse.

Informed by the scholarship of the processes of teaching and learning, contemporary reformers have taken direct aim at the assumption that factual and conceptual knowledge must precede more sophisticated forms of historical study. Instead, reformers stress that students must learn to think historically by doing—at a novice level—what expert historians do.[5]

With these ideas in mind, we thus propose an argument-based model for teaching the introductory history course. In the argument-based model, students participate in a contested, evidence-based discourse about the human past. In other words, students are asked to argue about history. And by arguing, students develop the dispositions and habits of mind that are central to the discipline of history.[6] As the former American Historical Association (AHA) president Kenneth Pomeranz noted in late 2013, historians should consider seeing general education history courses as valuable "not for the sake of 'general

---

3   See Lendol Calder, "Uncoverage: Toward a Signature Pedagogy for the History Survey," *Journal of American History* 92 (March 2006): 1358–1370; Joel M. Sipress and David J. Voelker, "The End of the History Survey Course: The Rise and Fall of the Coverage Model," *Journal of American History* 97 (March 2011): 1050–1066; and Penne Restad, "American History Learned, Argued, and Agreed Upon," in Michael Sweet and Larry K. Michaelson, eds., *Team-Based Learning in the Social Sciences and Humanities*, 159–180 (Sterling, VA: Stylus, 2012). For an overview of the Scholarship of Teaching and Learning (SoTL) in history, see Joel M. Sipress and David Voelker, "From Learning History to Doing History: Beyond the Coverage Model," in *Exploring Signature Pedagogies: Approaches to Teaching Disciplinary Habits of Mind*, pp. 19–35, edited by Regan Gurung, Nancy Chick, and Aeron Haynie (Stylus Publishing, 2008). Note also that the International Society for the Scholarship of Teaching and Learning in History was formed in 2006. See http://www.indiana.edu/~histsotl/blog/.

4   Calder, "Uncoverage," 1362–1363.

5   For influential critiques of the "facts first" assumption, see Sam Wineburg, "Crazy for History," *Journal of American History* 90 (March 2004), 1401–1414; and Calder, "Uncoverage."

6   For discussions of argument-based courses, see Barbara E. Walvoord and John R. Breihan, "Arguing and Debating: Breihan's History Course," in Barbara E. Walvoord and Lucille P. McCarthy, *Thinking and Writing in College: A Naturalistic Study of Students in Four Disciplines* (Urbana, IL: National Council of Teachers of English, 1990), 97–143; Todd Estes, "Constructing the Syllabus: Devising a Framework for Helping Students Learn to Think Like Historians," *History Teacher* 40 (February 2007), 183–201; Joel M. Sipress, "Why Students Don't Get Evidence and What We Can Do About It," *The History Teacher* 37 (May 2004), 351–363; and David J. Voelker, "Assessing Student Understanding in Introductory Courses: A Sample Strategy," *The History Teacher* 41 (August 2008): 505–518.

knowledge' but for the intellectual operations you can teach."[7] Likewise, the AHA "Tuning Project" defines the discipline in a way much more consistent with an argument-based course than with the coverage model:

> History is a set of evolving rules and tools that allows us to interpret the past with clarity, rigor, and an appreciation for interpretative debate. It requires evidence, sophisticated use of information, and a deliberative stance to explain change and continuity over time. As a profoundly public pursuit, history is essential to active and empathetic citizenship and requires effective communication to make the past accessible to multiple audiences. As a discipline, history entails a set of professional ethics and standards that demand peer review, citation, and toleration for the provisional nature of knowledge."[8]

We have designed *Debating American History* with these values in mind.

In the coverage-based model, historical knowledge is seen as an end in itself. In the argument-based model, by contrast, the historical knowledge that students must master serves as a body of evidence to be employed in argument and debate. While the ultimate goal of the coverage approach is the development of a kind of cultural literacy, the argument-based history course seeks to develop historical modes of thinking and to encourage students to incorporate these modes of thinking into their daily lives. Particularly when housed within a broader curriculum that emphasizes engaged learning, an argument-based course prepares students to ask useful questions in the face of practical problems and challenges—whether personal, professional, or civic. On encountering a historical claim, such as those that frequently arise in political discussions, they will know how to ask important questions about context, evidence, and logic. In this way, the argument-based course fulfills the discipline's longstanding commitment to the cultivation of engaged and informed citizens.[9]

While there is no single correct way to structure an argument-based course, such courses do share a number of defining characteristics that drive course design.[10] In particular, argument-based courses include these elements:

---

7   Kenneth Pomeranz, "Advanced History for Beginners: Why We Should Bring What's Best about the Discipline into the Gen Ed Classroom," *Perspectives on History* (November 2013), at http://www.historians.org/publications-and-directories/perspectives-on-history/november-2013/advanced-history-for-beginners-why-we-should-bring-whats-best-about-the-discipline-into-the-gen-ed-classroom.

8   This definition reflects the state of the Tuning Project as of September 2013. For more information, see "AHA History Tuning Project: 2013 History Discipline Core," at https://www.historians.org/teaching-and-learning/tuning-the-history-discipline/2013-history-discipline-core. Accessed January 31, 2019. This definition reflects the state of the Tuning Project as of September 2013. For more information, see "AHA History Tuning Project: History Discipline Core," at http://www.historians.org/teaching-and-learning/current-projects/tuning/history-discipline-core. Accessed March 8, 2014.

9   As recently as 2006, the AHA's Teaching Division reasserted the importance of history study and scholarship in the development of globally aware citizens. Patrick Manning, "Presenting History to Policy Makers: Three Position Papers," *Perspectives: The Newsmagazine of the American Historical Association* 44 (March 2006), 22–24.

10 Our approach to course design is deeply influenced by Grant Wiggins and Jay McTighe, *Understanding by Design*, 2nd ed. (Upper Saddle River, NJ: Pearson Education, 2006).

1. THEY ARE ORGANIZED AROUND SIGNIFICANT HISTORICAL QUESTIONS ABOUT WHICH HISTORIANS THEMSELVES DISAGREE.

Argument-based courses are, first and foremost, question-driven courses in which "big" historical questions (rather than simply topics or themes) provide the overall organizational structure. A "big" historical question is one about which historians themselves disagree and that has broad academic, intellectual, or cultural implications. Within these very broad parameters, the types of questions around which a course may be organized can vary greatly. The number of "big" questions addressed, however, must be relatively limited in number (perhaps three to five over the course of a typical fifteen-week semester), so that students can pursue the questions in depth.

2. THEY SYSTEMATICALLY EXPOSE STUDENTS TO RIVAL POSITIONS ABOUT WHICH THEY MUST MAKE INFORMED JUDGMENTS.

Argument-based courses systematically expose students to rival positions about which they must form judgments. Through repeated exploration of rival positions on a series of big questions, students see historical debate modeled in way that shatters any expectation that historical knowledge is clear-cut and revealed by authority. Students are thus confronted with the inescapable necessity to engage, consider, and ultimately evaluate the merits of a variety of perspectives.

3. THEY ASK STUDENTS TO JUDGE THE RELATIVE MERITS OF RIVAL POSITIONS ON BASIS OF HISTORICAL EVIDENCE.

To participate in historical argument, students must understand historical argument as more than a matter of mere opinion. For this to happen, students must learn to employ evidence as the basis for evaluating historical claims. Through being repeatedly asked to judge the relative merits of rival positions on the basis of evidence, students learn to see the relationship between historical evidence and historical assertions.

4. THEY REQUIRE STUDENTS TO DEVELOP THEIR OWN POSITIONS FOR WHICH THEY MUST ARGUE ON THE BASIS OF HISTORICAL EVIDENCE.

In an argument-based course, the ultimate aspiration should be for students to bring their own voices to bear on historical discourse in a way that is thoroughly grounded in evidence. Students must therefore have the opportunity to argue for their own positions. Such positions may parallel or synthesize those of the scholars with which they have engaged in the course or they may be original. In either case, though, students must practice applying disciplinary standards of evidence.

   Learning to argue about history is, above all, a process that requires students to develop new skills, dispositions, and habits of mind. Students develop these attributes through the act of arguing in a supportive environment where the instructor provides guidance and feedback. The instructor is also responsible for providing students with the background, context, and in-depth materials necessary both to fully understand and appreciate each big question and to serve as the body of evidence that forms the basis for judgments and arguments. While argument-based courses eschew any attempt to provide comprehensive coverage, they ask students to think deeply about a smaller number of historical questions—and in the process of arguing about the selected questions, students will develop significant content knowledge in the areas emphasized.

While a number of textbooks and readers in American history incorporate elements of historical argumentation, there are no published materials available that are specifically designed to support an argument-based course. *Debating American History* consists of a series of modular units, each focused on a specific topic and question in American history that will support all four characteristics of an argument-based course noted previously. Instructors will select units that support their overall course design, perhaps incorporating one or two modules into an existing course or structuring an entire course around three to five such units. (Instructors, of course, are free to supplement the modular units with other materials of their choosing, such as additional primary documents, secondary articles, multimedia materials, and book chapters.) By focusing on a limited number of topics, students will be able to engage in in-depth historical argumentation, including consideration of multiple positions and substantial bodies of evidence.

Each unit has the following elements:

1. THE BIG QUESTION

A brief narrative introduction that poses the central question of the unit and provides general background.

2. HISTORIANS' CONVERSATIONS

This section establishes the debate by providing two or three original essays that present distinct and competing scholarly positions on the Big Question. While these essays make occasional reference to major scholars in the field, they are not intended to provide historiographical overviews but rather to provide models of historical argumentation through the presentation and analysis of evidence.

3. DEBATING THE QUESTION

Each module includes a variety of materials containing evidence for students to use to evaluate the various positions and develop a position of their own. Materials may include primary source documents, images, a timeline, maps, or brief secondary sources. The specific materials vary depending on the nature of the question. Some modules include detailed case studies that focus on a particular facet of the Big Question.

For example, one module that we have developed for an early American history course focuses on the following Big Question: "How were the English able to displace the thriving Powhatan people from their Chesapeake homelands in the seventeenth century?" The Historians' Conversations section includes two essays: "Position #1: The Overwhelming Advantages of the English"; and "Position #2: Strategic Mistakes of the Powhatans." The unit materials allow students to undertake a guided exploration of both Powhatan and English motivations and strategies. The materials include two case studies that serve specific pedagogical purposes. The first case study asks the question, "Did Pocahontas Rescue John Smith from Execution?" Answering this question requires grappling with the nature of primary sources and weighing additional evidence from secondary sources; given historians' confidence that Powhatan did adopt Smith during his captivity, the case study also raises important questions about Powhatan strategy. The second case study focuses on the 1622 surprise attack that the Powhatans (led by Opechancanough) launched against the English, posing the question, "What Was the Strategy behind the 1622 Powhatan Surprise Attack?" Students wrestle with a number of scholarly perspectives regarding Opechancanough's purpose and the effectiveness of his strategy. Overall, this unit introduces students to the use of primary sources and the process of weighing different historical interpretations. Because of Disney's 1995 film *Pocahontas*, many students begin the unit thinking that they already know about the contact between the Powhatans and the English; many of them also savor the chance to bring critical, historical thinking to bear on this subject, and doing so deepens their understanding of how American Indians responded to European colonization.

Along similar lines, the Big Question for a module on the Gilded Age asks, "Why Was Industrialization in the Late Nineteenth Century Accompanied by Such Great Social and Political Turmoil?" The materials provided allow students to explore the labor conflicts of the period as well as the Populist revolt and to draw conclusions regarding the underlying causes of the social and political upheavals. Primary sources allow students to delve into labor conflicts from the perspectives of both workers and management and to explore both Populist and anti-Populist perspectives. Three short case studies allow students to examine specific instances of social conflict in depth. A body of economic data from the late nineteenth century is also included.

Many history instructors, when presented with the argument-based model, find its goals to be compelling, but they fear that it is overly ambitious—that introductory-level students will be incapable of engaging in historical thinking at an acceptable level. But, we must ask, how well do students learn under the coverage model? Student performance varies in an argument-based course, but it varies widely in a coverage-based course as well. In our experience, most undergraduate students are capable of achieving a basic-level competence at identifying and evaluating historical interpretations and using primary and secondary sources as evidence to make basic historical arguments. We not only have evidence of this success in the form of our own grade books, but we have studied our students' learning to document the success of our approach.[11] Students can indeed learn how to think like historians at a novice level, and in doing so they will gain both an appreciation for the discipline and develop a set of critical skills and dispositions that will contribute to their overall higher education. For this to happen, however, a course must be "backward designed" to promote and develop historical thinking. As historian Lawrence Gipson (Wabash College)

11 See Sipress, "Why Students Don't Get Evidence," and Voelker, "Assessing Student Understanding."

asked in a 1916 AHA discussion, "Will the student catch 'historical-mindedness' from his instructor like the mumps?"[12] The answer, clearly, is "no."

In addition to the modular units focused on big questions, instructors will also be provided with a brief instructors' manual, entitled "Developing an Argument-Based Course." This volume will provide instructors with guidance and advice on course development, as well as with sample in-class exercises and assessments. Additionally, each module includes an Instructor's Manual. Together, these resources will assist instructors with the process of creating an argument-based course, whether for a relatively small class at a liberal arts college or for a large class of students at a university. These resources can be used in both face-to-face and online courses.

The purpose of *Debating American History* is to provide instructors with both the resources and strategies that they will need to design such a course. This textbook alternative leaves plenty of room for instructor flexibility; and it requires instructors to carefully choose, organize, and introduce the readings to students, as well as to coach students through the process of thinking historically, even as they deepen their knowledge and understanding of particular eras and topics.

Joel M. Sipress
Professor of History,
University of Wisconsin-Superior

David J. Voelker
Associate Professor of Humanities and History,
University of Wisconsin-Green Bay

---

12 Lawrence H. Gipson, "Method of the Elementary Course in the Small College," *The History Teacher's Magazine* 8 (April 1917), 128. (The conference discussion took place in 1916.)

DEBATING AMERICAN HISTORY

INDUSTRIALIZATION AND SOCIAL CONFLICT
IN THE GILDED AGE

THE BIG QUESTION

WHY WAS INDUSTRIALIZATION IN THE LATE NINETEENTH CENTURY ACCOMPANIED BY SUCH GREAT SOCIAL AND POLITICAL TURMOIL?

Our bignesses—cities, factories, monopolies, fortunes, which are our empires, are the obesities of an age gluttonous beyond its powers of digestion. . . . Our size has got beyond both our science and our conscience.

–Henry Demarest Lloyd, *Wealth Against Commonwealth* (1894)

Employing nearly 4,000 people in the single-minded pursuit of steel production, the Homestead Steel Works, located just outside Pittsburgh, Pennsylvania, was a marvel of modern technology. Owned by Andrew Carnegie, the country's leading steelmaker, the mill symbolized America's emerging industrial might. In July of 1892, however, Homestead was the site of a violent confrontation that came to symbolize the chaos and turmoil that accompanied America's late nineteenth-century industrial boom. On the morning of July 6th, a force of 300 private Pinkerton security guards employed by the Carnegie Steel Company landed on the banks of the Monongahela River in an effort to retake the steelworks from striking workers who had blocked access to the facility. The Pinkertons were met by a crowd of strikers and their supporters, many of them armed, intent on stopping them. No one knows who fired the first shot, but the firefight that followed left several dead on both sides, with even more injured. The Pinkertons remained besieged for the rest of the day, until the early evening, when they surrendered and were taken prisoner. The strikers' success was short-lived, though. On July 12, a large force of state militia arrived in Homestead. With the mill under armed protection, the steel company was able to bring in replacement workers and restart production.

The rapid rise of the steel industry was just one indication of America's industrial transformation. In 1870, the United States was a primarily agricultural society. By 1920, the country was the world's leading industrial powerhouse. As industrialization accelerated after the Civil War, observers were astounded by the speed and the scope of the changes that they witnessed. The late nineteenth century saw breathtaking growth in traditional manufacturing, such as textiles, clothing, and shoemaking, along with the emergence of entirely new industries like steelmaking and petroleum—industries that would help define the modern economy of the twentieth-century. "One can hardly believe there has been a revolution in history so rapid, so extensive, so complete," declared philosopher John Dewey.[1] Between 1870 and 1920, the value of all goods and services produced in the United States per person doubled. And in 1920, the United States census found that, for the first time, the majority of Americans lived in urban areas.

The nation's industrial transformation allowed for the production of material goods on a scale unimaginable to earlier generations. Some observers maintained that modern technology and mass production would free humanity from the material deprivation that had long haunted it. "Better morals, better sanitary conditions, better health, better wages; these are the practical results of the factory system," wrote the head of the Massachusetts Bureau of Statistics of Labor in 1882.[2] Others, however, worried about the vast extremes of wealth and poverty that industrialization fostered. Some even feared that concentrated corporate wealth threatened the very foundations of American democracy. The system of corporate life, wrote Charles Francis Adams Jr. (grandson and great-grandson of presidents), is "a new power, for which our language contains no name. We know what aristocracy, autocracy, democracy are; but we have no word to express government by monied corporations."[3]

The great industrial boom of the late nineteenth century was accompanied by a wave of social strife and political turmoil. A nationwide railroad strike in July 1877 that left dead over 100 people, mainly striking workers and their supporters, set the tone. The strike took place in the midst of a painful economic depression that cost hundreds of thousands their jobs while threatening the profits and the very survival of many businesses. (The late nineteenth-century boom was interrupted by a series of sharp economic downturns.) When financially strained railroad corporations sought to save money by slashing employee wages and increasing workloads, thousands of railroad workers spontaneously walked off the job, bringing much of the nation's transportation system to a halt. In cities such as Baltimore and Pittsburgh, the arrival of state militia troops (which in some cases opened fire on crowds of strikers and sympathizers) sparked riots that left scores dead and resulted in mass destruction of railroad property. Two weeks after the initial walkouts, the strikes had been crushed and the trains were running again.

The highest profile labor conflicts of the era, such as the 1892 Homestead Strike and Pullman Boycott of 1894, in which railroad workers again brought much of the country's rail traffic to a halt, are memorialized in the history books. Countless other strikes and conflicts, touching cities and towns throughout the country, are all but forgotten. Between 1881 and 1890, the federal Bureau of Labor Statistics estimated that there were nearly 10,000 work stoppages nationwide. In 1886 alone, over 600,000 individuals (about one out of every ten non-farm workers) either walked off the job or were locked out by employers in labor disputes.[4] Many of these disputes ended in violence and bloodshed. In the summer of

---

1   Dewey quoted in Eric Foner, *Give Me Liberty! An American History* (New York: W.W. Norton, 2009), 558.
2   Quoted in Alan Trachtenberg, *The Incorporation of America: Culture and Society in the Gilded Age* (New York: Hill and Wang, 1982), 42.
3   Charles Francis Adams, *A Chapter of Erie* (Boston: Fields, Osgood, and Company, 1869), 150.
4   Melvyn Dubofsky, *Industrialism and the American Worker, 1865–1920*, 3rd ed. (Wheeling, IL: Harlan Davidson, 1996), 39–40.

1889, for instance, workers constructing streets and sewers in Duluth, Minnesota, walked off the job to protest a reduction in wages. As workers marched from work site to work site urging others to join them, they found themselves involved in a series of skirmishes with local police that culminated in an armed clash in which a number of strikers were seriously wounded and one bystander was killed. When a similar strike broke out shortly thereafter in neighboring Superior, Wisconsin, the governor of the state declared martial law and dispatched a company of state militia troops to occupy the community. Communities across the country witnessed similar strife and turmoil throughout the period. In the late nineteenth century, in fact, the United States had the most violent labor relations of any country in the world.

In many of the country's emerging industries, workers sought to create labor unions so that, through concerted action, they could gain leverage in their negotiations with employers. Outside of a handful of skilled trades, though, most efforts to organize and sustain unions ended in failure. Oftentimes, employers simply refused to recognize or negotiate with unions, and unskilled and semi-skilled workers lacked the means to compel employers to the bargaining table, particularly given the ease with which companies could find new workers to replace those who went out on strike. There were also broader efforts to reform the workplace. In 1886, for instance, workers in many cities organized protests and strikes in an unsuccessful effort to institute an eight-hour work day. The largest labor reform organization of the period was the Knights of Labor. The Knights aimed to unite all workers, regardless of skill or occupation, in a single, nation-wide, labor reform organization. Founded in 1869 in the city of Philadelphia, the Knights grew slowly through the 1870s and early 1880s. Following a successful 1885 strike against New York financier Jay Gould's railroad system, the Knights' membership skyrocketed from 100,000 to more than 700,000 in a matter of months. "Never in all history has there been such a spectacle as the march of the Order of the Knights of Labor at the present time," wrote the editor of one labor newspaper.[5] The year 1886, however, marked the peak of the Knights as an organization. In that year, the Knights were defeated in a series of high profile strikes (including another dispute with Gould), and the organization soon fell into decline.

Many farmers, particularly cotton farmers in the South and wheat farmers on the Great Plains, also protested what they saw as the injustices of the emerging industrial order. A painful decline in the prices of agricultural commodities in the late nineteenth century led to rising debt levels among farmers that spread fears of farm foreclosure and loss of land. Farmers in the South and West complained that while agriculture languished, the captains of finance on New York's Wall Street and the railroad barons grew wealthy at their expense. In response, southern and western farmers came together through organizations with names like the Grange and the Agricultural Wheel to engage in collective action designed to improve their conditions. The largest such effort was the National Farmers' Alliance, an agricultural organization that swept the South and West in the late 1880s with a promise to lift farmers out of poverty and debt through the collective marketing of farm products and collective purchasing of supplies. When economic cooperation proved

---

5   Quoted in Melvyn Dubofsky and Foster Rhea Dulles, *Labor in America: A History*, 6th ed. (Wheeling, Illinois: Harlan Davidson, 1999), 130.

inadequate to address the farmers' plight, the Alliance rallied behind a series of reform proposals designed to address the injustices of the nation's financial and transportation systems.

To address the plight of farmers, the Alliance proposed that certain financial and transportation institutions should be placed under government control and operated in the public interest rather than for private profit. Alliancemen (a nickname for Alliance members) called for the railroads to be taken out of private hands and be placed under public ownership. This, they argued, would put an end to the excessive rates farmers were charged to ship their products. The Alliance also proposed a government run "sub-treasury" that would provide farmers with low interest agricultural loans to free them from dependence on private banks and creditors. Alliancemen blamed falling agricultural prices on the failure of the nation's money supply to keep pace with its rapidly growing economy and demanded that the supply of money be expanded by shifting from a gold-backed to a silver-backed currency or by dispensing entirely with the idea that money must be backed by precious metals. Opponents of the Alliance derided their proposals as "socialism" and warned that abandoning the gold standard would undermine the integrity of the nation's financial system.

When the major political parties (the Democrats and Republicans) refused to embrace the demands of the Farmers' Alliance, reformers established their own political party, the People's Party (also known as the Populist Party). Populists hoped to unite farmers and workers in a coalition that would sweep the old parties from power and usher in an age of social and economic reform. As farmers in the South and West flocked to the People's Party, the Populist upsurge threw the country's existing two-party system into turmoil. The People's Party, however, had trouble reaching beyond its core constituency among cotton and wheat farmers who had participated in the Farmers' Alliance movement. Although Populism was among the largest third-party movements in US History, the People's Party failed to achieve its goal of displacing the Democrats and Republicans. In 1896, the Democratic Party (fearing the loss of support to the rapidly growing People's Party) nominated Senator William Jennings Bryan for President on a platform that embraced the Populist call for a silver-backed currency. (Bryan lost the presidential election to Republican William McKinley.) With the Democrats newly positioned as the party of "reform," the People's Party began to unravel. The labor and agricultural reforms that they championed, however, continued to be important issues for years to come.

Historians have long debated why industrialization in the late nineteenth century was accompanied by such unrest among farmers and workers. For some, the conflicts of the time simply represent the difficulties of adjustment to the new ways of living and working associated with industrialization. Others, by contrast, argue that the turmoil of the period reflects deeper divisions and inequalities inherent in industrial society. Did the upheavals of the period reflect fundamental divisions within the United States, or were these merely the growing pains of a new social and economic order? By asking why industrialization was accompanied by such great unrest, we may gain a better understanding of how farmers and workers experienced this period of rapid change. We may also gain insights into the nature of the modern industrial system that still shapes our lives today.

TIMELINE

1873
Global financial panic leads to painful economic depression that lasts until late 1870s

1886
Workers engage in nationwide protest for an eight-hour workday; protests in Chicago and Milwaukee end in bloodshed

1887
The National Farmers' Alliance launches an organizing campaign that brings hundreds of thousands of southern farmers into the organization.

1873
Andrew Carnegie introduces the Bessemer process for mass production of steel to the United States

1886
Membership in the Knights of Labor peaks at over 700,000

1891
Members of Farmers' Alliance, the Knights of Labor, and other labor and agrarian organizations form the People's Party (also known as the Populist Party)

1877
Nationwide railroad strike leads to deadliest labor conflict in US history

1886
Formation of the American Federation of Labor as a national federation of trade unions

1892

The People's Party holds its first national convention and adopts the Omaha Platform as its reform manifesto

1893

Financial panic on Wall Street; economic depression brings high unemployment and sends prices for farm commodities below the price of production

1894

Boycott of Pullman railroad cars in labor dispute leads to national rail strike; US Army sent in to break the strike

1892

Strike at Andrew Carnegie's Homestead steelworks ends in bloodshed

1894

People's Party makes gains in state and federal elections

1896

Democratic Party nominates William Jennings Bryan for president on a reform platform; Bryan defeated and the People's Party collapses

HISTORIANS' CONVERSATIONS

POSITION #1—A TIME OF TURMOIL
Class War in Industrializing America

"This association of poverty with progress is the great enigma of our times," wrote social reformer Henry George in 1879. "It is the central fact from which spring industrial, social, and political difficulties that perplex the world, and with which statesmanship and philanthropy and education grapple in vain." The nineteenth-century, George noted, had been marked by astounding growth in the productive capacity of humankind. "The utilization of steam and electricity, the introduction of improved processes and labor-saving machinery, the greater subdivision and grander scale of production, the wonderful facilitation of exchanges, have multiplied enormously the effectiveness of labor," he observed.[1] This material progress had not, however, served to improve the conditions of life for the toiling masses. Instead, the benefits of progress had flowed mainly to a handful of captains of industry who had amassed historically unprecedented fortunes. Meanwhile, George noted, millions struggled to achieve even the barest of existences.

In late nineteenth-century America, many of those who labored on farms and in industrial settings came to similar conclusions as George. And as they did, they joined together to address the inequities of the industrial age. Workers formed labor organizations to bargain with employers for better conditions and to lobby government for workplace regulations, such as the eight-hour day. Farmers also banded together into associations, both to gain economic leverage against railroads and creditors and to push for government policies favorable to agriculture. In the end, though, the very economic inequalities that had driven farmers and workers to action proved their undoing. The concentrated wealth of railroads, banks, and other corporate entities gave them the power to resist the demands of farmers and workers and to directly influence government policy. Confronted by an unholy alliance of corporate wealth and the state, protests for economic justice grew increasingly militant and the demands for change became more radical. The result was an extended period of social and political turmoil—a class war between those who labored and the owners of concentrated corporate wealth.

In 1860, the United States was an agrarian nation in which at least half of all adults were self-employed on farms or in artisan shops. (The enslaved workers of the American South were, of course, the great exception.) Over the next two generations, though, the

---

1   Henry George, *Progress and Poverty: An Inquiry into the Cause of Industrial Depressions, and of Increase of Want with Increase of Wealth*, 4th ed. (New York: D. Appleton and Company, 1886), 9, 3.

United States was transformed into a modern industrial nation in which the vast majority worked for wages. The emerging industrial economy was dominated by the corporation, a new form of business organization that allowed production on a scale unimaginable in earlier times. The first of the great corporations were the railroads that stitched together previously isolated communities into an integrated national economy. The railroad magnates were also the first to accumulate vast corporate fortunes, as epitomized by that of Cornelius Vanderbilt, the owner of the New York Central Railroad, who by the time of his death in 1877 had amassed a historically unprecedented estate of $100 million. In the period after the Civil War, men such as Andrew Carnegie and John D. Rockefeller applied forms of corporate organization to industries such as steel making and oil to build vast business empires that came to dominate both the economy and the political system.

The emerging corporate economy created disparities of wealth and power on a scale that had previously been seen in the United States only on the slave-based plantations of the pre–Civil War South. In the cities, a great working class took shape that owned little or no property and that worked long hours in dangerous conditions for what historian Melvyn Dubofsky terms "a meager existence."[2] With a typical work week well in excess of fifty hours, and with one of the highest industrial accident rates in the world, the late nineteenth-century American workplace was brutal, leaving an average of 35,000 workers dead annually in the 1880s. Although industrial wages, adjusted for inflation, did gradually increase between 1870 and 1900, they kept pace with neither the growing productivity of labor nor the rising fortunes of the wealthy. The late nineteenth century also saw a series of painful economic downturns (about one per decade) that sent unemployment skyrocketing at a time when few if any public resources existed to help sustain those who were thrown out of work. In the countryside, farmers also found themselves increasingly subject to the domination of corporate organizations. Where formerly farmers had been largely self-sufficient and had produced primarily to meet their own needs and those of local and regional markets, they now found themselves incorporated into a national economy that left them dependent on railroads (and the shipping rates they imposed) to send their goods to market. Ironically, the very productivity of American agriculture, which allowed it to sustain a growing urban population, also led to a glut of farm products that sent the prices received by farmers spiraling downward. Over time, more and more farmers became dependent on banks and other lenders to finance their operations. In the context of falling prices, this dangerous dependence on borrowing raised the specter of bankruptcy, foreclosure, and loss of land.

The political clout of corporate America was exemplified by the power of the railroads. Railroad corporations purchased influence over lawmakers in both the Democratic and Republican parties through direct cash payments and distributions of corporate stock, neither of which was barred by law at the time. The railroads also provided legislators at the state and federal level with passes for free passenger travel. The funds invested in the political process paid handsome dividends for the railroads in the form of lavish subsidies for the construction of new lines. Over the course the nineteenth century, railroads received

---

2   Melvyn Dubofsky, *Industrialization and the American Worker, 1865–1920* (Arlington Heights, Illinois: AHM Publishing Company, 1975), 19.

over $700 million in cash and over 100 million acres of land to support new construction. The land grants far exceeded what was needed to actually construct new lines; the railroads sold the excess acres to settlers and land speculators to earn additional cash. Railroads and other corporations also had close personal ties to political leaders in both major parties. The 1884 Republican Presidential nominee James G. Blaine, for instance, was closely connected to the railroads; and Republican Senator John C. Spooner of Wisconsin was himself a prominent railroad attorney. Democratic President Grover Cleveland chose railroad lawyer Richard Olney as his attorney general. William Whitney, one of Cleveland's top political advisors and a member of his cabinet, was a millionaire corporate attorney who had married into the Standard Oil fortune.

The conditions of industrial life gave birth to the country's first labor movement, as workers came together to form unions, political parties, and other organizations. At first, much of the movement's energy was geared toward government regulation of the workplace. Workers in many states lobbied for such measures as limits on the hours of work, government inspection of factory safety, and prohibitions against child labor. (At the time, the dominant interpretation of the US Constitution barred the federal government from directly regulating the workplace.) In May 1886, hundreds of thousands of striking workers and their supporters held protests nationwide in support of the eight-hour day. A number of states did enact pro-worker laws, but the impact was minimal, as enforcement was spotty. In many cases, courts actually overturned workplace regulations. In the absence of federal labor legislation, workplace regulation remained a patchwork of weak and ineffective state and local laws.

Eventually, many labor leaders, including Samuel Gompers of the American Federation of Labor, despaired of improving the conditions of work through government intervention and instead encouraged direct workplace action to compel employers to make improvements. Here too, however, workers faced enormous obstacles. Repeatedly, workers banded together either informally or formally in unions to bargain collectively over wages, hours, and working conditions only to face stubborn resistance from employers who refused to even negotiate. In response, workers repeatedly walked off the jobs in efforts to bring employers to the bargaining table. Sometimes employers agreed to talk, particularly where workers had skills that were in high demand. Often, though, companies simply replaced striking workers, which was relatively easy to do, especially when the work was unskilled or when unemployment was high. The result was a series of bitter and often violent labor disputes that rocked communities across the nation, as strikes escalated into battles over physical control of the workplace. Faced with the prospect of being replaced, strikers sought to bring work to halt through direct mob action. Employers responded with force, either in the form of private security guards, local police, state militia, or in the case of the 1894 Pullman railroad boycott, federal troops. Unions also faced hostility from courts, who, in a series of cases, declared the tactic of withdrawing labor to be an illegal restraint against trade. In the case of the Pullman railroad boycott, American Railway Union President Eugene Debs spent six months in prison after defying a back-to-work order from a federal court.

Farmers who hoped to improve their economic conditions also faced bitter resistance from corporate interests and their representatives in government. Like workers, farmers in the late nineteenth century banded together in associations that engaged in both direct action and in lobbying the government for economic reforms. The Grange, a farm organization founded in the 1870s, for instance, fought for government regulation of the rates that railroads could charge to ship products and also pursued cooperative marketing of goods in order to gain better terms for its members. The largest and most influential agricultural organizations of the late nineteenth century was the National Farmers' Alliance, which in the late 1880s and early 1890s recruited over a million members, mainly in the South and the West. At first, the Alliance directed its energies primarily to cooperative purchasing and marketing, an effort that culminated in efforts to free its members from dependence on private banks and lenders through the development of cooperative credit. Eventually, the Alliance concluded that the power of the railroads and financiers was simply too great to be overcome with voluntary cooperation alone. The Alliance thus proposed a program of sweeping economic reforms that included taking the railroads out of private hands and placing them under public ownership and the development of what they called a government "sub-treasury" that would provide low-interest government loans to help farmers finance their operations.

The Alliance's vision of a more egalitarian social order in which railroads, banks, and other corporations would be subject to public control brought it into direct conflict with the established political parties and the powerful economic interests that they represented. The refusal of Democratic and Republican politicians to embrace the demands of the Farmers' Alliance inspired members of the organization to found their own political party—the People's Party (also known as the Populist Party). In the election of 1892, Populist presidential candidate James B. Weaver carried five western states and had a strong showing in a number of states in the South. The party also elected eleven members of Congress as well as governors in Kansas, North Dakota, and Colorado. If not for a wave of violence and electoral fraud directed against it in much of the South, the Populists would have had even more success in their initial effort as a national party. In 1893, a financial panic on Wall Street sparked the most painful economic depression of the late nineteenth century. As agricultural prices plummeted to all-time lows, new support came to the People's Party. As the 1896 election approached, optimistic Populists hoped to displace the Democrats as one of the nation's two major parties.

As historian Lawrence Goodwyn argues, the Populist movement offered a moment of "democratic promise," as millions of Americans imagined the possibility of a more inclusive and egalitarian alternative to an emerging corporate order characterized by vast inequalities of wealth and power.[3] In the end, however, the Populists simply lacked the resources to succeed as a national party. Based in the agricultural regions of the South and West, the party had limited success reaching out to the nation's growing urban working class. In the South, political violence and electoral theft took a heavy toll on the party. In 1896, the Democratic Party stole much of the Populists' thunder by nominating Congressman William Jennings Bryan of Nebraska for president on the platform of moderate economic reform; and soon after, the People's Party collapsed as a political organization.

---

3   Lawrence Goodwyn, *Democratic Promise: The Populist Moment in America* (New York: Oxford University Press, 1976).

Frightened by even the watered-down Populism of William Jennings Bryan, corporate interests showered the presidential campaign of Republican candidate William McKinley with a flood of donations that helped deliver the White House to McKinley. Powerful economic forces retained their grip on the country's political system. The moment of "democratic promise" had passed.

As the twentieth century dawned, the United States stood poised to become the world's great industrial powerhouse. Unresolved, however, was the place that those who labored would occupy within the new industrial order. For over a generation, farmers and workers had struggled to achieve a measure of respect, dignity, and security, only to suffer defeat at the hands of concentrated corporate power and its allies within government. As Melvyn Dubofsky writes, "the power of the productive forces of the economy" had "surpassed the ability of human institutions to control them more equitably." The result was what Dubofsky calls a "time of chaos."[4] The outright class warfare of the late nineteenth-century has long since been left behind. Nevertheless, the questions first raised in that era, of whether democracy can coexist with concentrated corporate wealth and whether those who labor will fully reap the benefits of modern industry, still remain.

---

4   Dubofsky, *American Worker*, 31, 29.

POSITION #2—BIRTH PANGS
OF THE MODERN AGE
Cultural Change and Social Conflict
in Industrializing America

The labor radicals and Populists of the late nineteenth century believed themselves to be part of an epic struggle in which the future of American democracy and perhaps even the fate of mankind were at stake. "We meet in the midst of a nation brought to the verge of moral, political, and material ruin," bemoaned the People's Party's 1892 Omaha Platform. "The fruits of the toil of millions are boldly stolen to build up colossal fortunes for a few, unprecedented in the history of mankind; and the possessors of these, in turn, despise the republic and endanger liberty." Were a different path not chosen, warned the Populists, America would soon become a nation of "tramps and millionaires." This prophecy was compelling to many, and in light of the real economic deprivation of the time, its appeal is understandable.

Nonetheless, the portrait of a late nineteenth-century America embroiled in class war, a portrait embraced by some historians, is overdrawn. True, the conditions of work and life were harsh for the emerging industrial working class. Yet, despite periodic bouts of economic recession and joblessness, the real purchasing power of most workers' wages gradually increased over the period. Cotton and wheat farmers did struggle with declining prices and high-levels of debt, and there were individual cases of foreclosure and land loss. The massive and widespread pauperization of farmers that many feared, though, never took place. In fact, following the brutal economic depression of the mid 1890s, agricultural prices rebounded and the economic position of family farmers stabilized. The nation was indeed rocked by a series of tumultuous labor conflicts and protest movements, but only a fraction of the population participated in these battles. Outside of a handful of wheat and cotton producing states, for instance, the People's Party struggled to gain a following; and even on its home turf, its period of influence was quite brief. "Industrialization drove some people to despair," writes historian Harold Livesay, "some to rebellion, and some back to the old country, but most tolerated it because it gave them hope for a better life for their children, if not for themselves."[1]

---

1   Harold C. Livesay, *American Made: Men Who Shaped the American Economy* (Boston: Little, Brown, and Company, 1979), 7.

What then explains the unease and turmoil of this period of rapid industrialization? The answer is to be found in the cultural impact of industrialization. We often think of the industrial revolution as a process of technological development whose most significant impact was an increase in the productive capacity of humankind. Industrialization, however, involves far more than a simple change in the methods of economic production. Rather, the rise of modern industry reshaped the very fabric of daily life and fostered new cultural values and practices. For those who lived through these transformations, the process could be gut-wrenching, as old ways of life fell by the wayside to be replaced by new ways that could feel unfamiliar, alien, and even oppressive. It was "the hardships and maladjustments arising from rapid economic change," to use Edward C. Kirkland's phrase, that led to the tumult of the period.[2]

Imagine, for instance, what first generation industrial workers experienced as they made the transition from the old to the new. Most of those who went to work in the nation's factories, mines, and on its railroads were products of pre-modern agrarian cultures. Between 1870 and 1920, about eleven million Americans moved from farm to city. Millions more came from the European countryside, with smaller numbers arriving from rural parts of Asia and Latin America. The fabric of daily life in these lands of origins, despite their enormous geographic diversity, had certain features in common that marked them as distinctive from a modern industrial society. In pre-modern agrarian cultures, life is governed by the natural cycles of seasons and the daily cycle of dusk and dawn. The fruits of one's labor are immediately visible with a direct relationship between the work one does and the production of the basic necessities of life. The modern world, by contrast, is governed by bureaucratic rules that determine when one must rise, where one must be, what one must do and how one must do it, and for how long. Family, leisure, and work are thoroughly intertwined in an agrarian culture, with the household serving both as the fundamental social unit and the location of economic production. Industrialization severs labor from the rest of life and assigns it to specialized workplaces that lack the close bonds of family and community that characterized work in the pre-modern era. Survival in the pre-industrial world required intense physical labor, but that labor was largely self-regulated and involved cooperation among family and neighbors. The typical modern experience of selling one's labor to an often-times anonymous employer in exchange for a wage was a largely alien concept.

It is important not to romanticize the conditions of life in the pre-industrial era. Much of the world's peasant farming classes eked out a marginal existence on small plots of land only to face the unpredictable and deadly scourges of drought, famine, and disease. Nevertheless, for those who were a product of pre-modern agrarian cultures, the emerging modern world could seem cold, alien, and unforgiving. In his classic study of European immigrants to the United States, Oscar Handlin writes of the "uprooted" who were torn out of "traditional, accustomed environments" and replanted on "strange ground" where they were compelled to work out "new relationships, new meanings to their lives,

---

2   Edward C. Kirkland, "Rhetoric and Rage Over the Division of Wealth in the Eighteen Nineties," *Proceedings of the American Antiquarian Society* 79 (October 1969), 243.

often under harsh and hostile circumstances."[3] Whether newly arrived from the Italian or Chinese countryside, or from rural Iowa or Alabama, many first-generation industrial workers found a modern workplace characterized by bosses, clocks, and schedules to be both strange and oppressive. Historian Herbert Gutman locates the source of the social turmoil of the period in the tension between traditional agrarian cultures and values and the demands imposed by the "regularities and disciplines" of the industrial workplace.[4] Some workers responded through strikes and protests. Others abandoned industrial life, with an estimated one-third of European immigrants returning to the old country. The early labor movement gave voice to the unease many felt through its calls to abolish the "wage system." Over time, however, early industrial workers (and more importantly their children and grandchildren) gradually adapted to the rhythms and the ways of the modern world.

Those who remained in the American countryside also felt the alienation produced by rapid cultural change. James Turner, in his study of the Populist movement, concludes that economic hardship, though a catalyst for the farmers' movement, was not its underlying cause. Supporters of the Farmers' Alliance and People's Party, Turner found, were not necessarily those in greatest economic distress. Rather, it was those who lived in the greatest social isolation that were most inclined to rebel against the emerging industrial order. Farmers had long been hailed as the backbone of the nation, with the agrarian way of life held up as a model of democratic virtue. Thomas Jefferson considered those who tilled the soil to be "the chosen people of God"; and even Alexander Hamilton, the great apostle of industrial and commercial development, once wrote that agriculture "has intrinsically a strong claim to pre-eminence over every other kind of industry."[5] By the late nineteenth century, however, status and authority was increasingly flowing to urban professionals and entrepreneurs whose position rested on personal wealth and formal education. Perhaps more galling, this new urban elite scoffed at physical labor, particularly the rural labor that produced the very stuff of life that made urban existence possible. "The felt differences between backwoods farmers and other Americans were growing sharper, isolation becoming more awkward, even painful, the sense of being left out deepening," writes Turner.[6] It was those most removed both culturally and geographically from the emerging industrial world, argues Turner, who felt the greatest resentment. It was this resentment that fed the farmers' movement.

By the twentieth century, Americans were learning to adjust to the realities of modern industrial life. Unlike their parents and grandparents, second- and third-generation industrial workers were themselves a product of the industrial order, having been

---

3   Oscar Handlin, *The Uprooted: The Epic Story of the Great Migrations That Made the American People* (Boston: Little, Brown, 1951), 5.

4   Herbert G. Gutman, "Work, Culture, and Society in Industrializing America, 1815–1919," in *Work, Culture, and Society in Industrializing America* (New York: Knopf, 1976), 13.

5   Thomas Jefferson, *Notes on the State of Virginia* (Boston: Lilly and Wait, 1832), 172. (Originally published in 1785); Alexander Hamilton, *Report on Manufactures* (Washington, DC: United States Department of Treasury, 1913), 5. (Originally published in 1791)

6   James Turner, "Understanding the Populists," *Journal of American History* 67 (September 1980), 371.

socialized into a world of clocks, schedules, and bureaucratic rules by years of experience in institutions of public education. At the same time, there was growing awareness among all social classes of the need to put in place policies to address the harsher features of industrial life. Beginning with the Progressive Era of the early twentieth century and continuing through the New Deal period of the 1930s, a series of reforms were enacted that gradually replaced the jungle-like atmosphere of the early industrial economy with a more stable and predictable marketplace. Financial regulations softened the harsh cycle of economic boom and bust, while workplace regulations such as the minimum wage, limits on the hours of work, and safety requirements provided important protections to workers. Though the rivalry among competing economic interests remains a notable feature modern American politics, these conflicts have generally been resolved without the turmoil and violence that characterized the late nineteenth century.

The rapid social changes of the late nineteenth century laid the foundation for the United States to become the dominant political, military, and economic superpower of the twentieth century. And, despite persistent inequalities with which we struggle to this day, the industrial system symbolized by men like Andrew Carnegie and John D. Rockefeller, would provide twentieth-century Americans with a standard of living that became the envy of much of the world. In terms of life expectancy, levels of nutrition, and other measures of material comfort, the modern American working class achieved a quality of life that was unprecedented by the standards of the pre-industrial world. Industrialization produced its share of millionaires. Fears that those who labored would be reduced to the level of tramps, however, were misplaced.

Nevertheless, for those who lived through the age of industrialization, the promise of future material prosperity could not erase the unease produced by the loss of traditional values. A more rigid, structured, bureaucratic, and individualistic world was indeed the price of material progress. Yet, as historian Glenn Porter points out, this was a price that most Americans were eventually willing to pay. "The passage of time gradually made the new institutions of the large corporation more familiar and less threatening than it had seemed when it first appeared on the scene," writes Porter. "Industrialization did mean, as so many had feared, the slow atrophy of agrarian and rural influences on the culture. Most of the country, however, soon forgot such worries and embraced the pleasures of an industrial, urban, and suburban civilization."[7] The birth of this new social order was extremely painful for those who lived through it; but in the case of industrializing America, the pain proved largely transitory.

---

7   Glenn Porter, "Industrialization and the Rise of Big Business," in Charles C. Calhoun, ed., *The Gilded Age: Essays on the Origins of Modern America* (Wilmington, Delaware: SR Books, 1996), 16.

DEBATING THE QUESTION

PRIMARY SOURCES ON LABOR

The documents in this section provide insights into the labor conflicts of the age of industrialization from a variety of perspectives. The sources include materials produced by workers, by employers, and by labor organizations. A federal court decision that limited the rights of unions and a newspaper advertisement urging individuals to purchase firearms for personal protection are also included. When working with these sources, focus on what they reveal about the viewpoints that people from a variety of backgrounds brought to the workplace issues of the late nineteenth century. What might they tell us about why workers and employers so often clashed during age of industrialization?

1.1 EXCERPT FROM INTERNATIONAL HARVESTER BROCHURE (1912)

In 1912, the International Harvester Company (a major manufacturer of farm machinery based in Chicago) produced a brochure designed to teach its immigrant Polish workers English. International Harvester's Polish workers had relatively little experience with industrial work and were generally hired for unskilled job. As you read the first lesson in the brochure, think about what it is the company is *really* trying to teach its immigrant workers.

GUIDING QUESTIONS:

1. Why do you think the company would choose these items for its first lesson in English?
2. The stated purpose of this brochure was to teach the English language. What else was the company trying to teach its workforce?

EXCERPT FROM INTERNATIONAL HARVESTER BROCHURE

LESSON ONE—GENERAL (1912)

I hear the whistle. I must hurry.
I hear the five minute whistle.
It is time to go into the shop.
I take my check from the gate board and hang it on the department board.
I change my clothes and get ready to work.
The starting whistle blows.
I eat my lunch.
It is forbidden to eat until then.
The whistle blows at five minutes of starting time.

I get ready to go to work.
I work until the whistle blows to quit.
I leave my place nice and clean.
I put all my clothes in my locker.
I go home.

DRAWING CONCLUSIONS

1. What does this document suggest about how International Harvester's management viewed its immigrant workforce?
2. What can we learn from this document about the sources of conflict between workers and employers during the age of industrialization?

From Gerd Korman, "Americanization at the Factory Gate," *Industrial and Labor Relations Review* 18 (April 1965), 402.

1.2 MORRIS ROSENFELD, "IN THE FACTORY" (1914)

Morris Rosenfeld was a Jewish immigrant who worked in the clothing industry of New York City. In the late nineteenth century, he gained some notoriety as a poet, writing primarily in the Yiddish language (the language spoken by much of Europe's Jewish population). In this poem, he describes the experience of working in a clothing factory.

GUIDING QUESTIONS:

1. What, according to Rosenfeld, was it like working in a clothing factory?
2. How, according to Rosenfeld, did it *feel* to work in a clothing factory?
3. Why do you think working in a clothing factory felt this way to Rosenfeld?

IN THE FACTORY

By Morris Rosenfeld
[Originally published in Yiddish with English prose translation in 1898. This is a 1914 verse translation.]

Oh, here in the shop the machines roar so wildly,
That oft, unaware that I am, or have been,
I sink and am lost in the terrible tumult;
And void is my soul . . . I am but a machine.
I work and I work and I work, never ceasing;
Create and create things from morning till e'en;
For what?—and for whom—Oh, I know not!
   Oh, ask not!
Who ever has heard of a conscious machine?
No, here is no feeling, no thought and no reason;
This life-crushing labor has ever supprest
The noblest and finest, the truest and richest,
The deepest, the highest and humanly best.
The seconds, the minutes, they pass out forever,
They vanish, swift fleeting like straws in a gale.
I drive the wheel madly as tho' to o'ertake them,—
Give chase without wisdom, or wit, or avail.
The clock in the workshop,—it rests not a moment;

It points on, and ticks on: Eternity—Time;
And once someone told me the clock had a
   meaning,—
Its pointing and ticking had reason and rhyme.
And this too he told me,—or had I been
   dreaming,—
The clock wakened life in one, forces unseen,
And something besides; . . . I forget what;
   Oh, ask not!
I know not, I know not, I am a machine.
At times, when I listen, I hear the clock plainly;—
The reason of old—the old meaning—is gone!
The maddening pendulum urges me forward
To labor and labor and still labor on.
The tick of the clock is the Boss in his anger!
The face of the clock has the eyes of a foe;
The clock—Oh, I shudder—dost hear how it
   drives me?
It calls me "Machine!" and it cries to me "Sew!"
At noon, when about me the wild tumult ceases,
And gone is the master, and I sit apart,
And dawn in my brain is beginning to glimmer,
The wound comes agape at the core of my heart;

From Morris Rosenfeld, *Songs of Labor and Other Poems*, trans. Rose Pastor Stokes and Helena Frank (Boston: R.G. Badger, 1914), 7–9.

And tears, bitter tears flow; ay, tears that are scalding;
They moisten my dinner—my dry crust of bread;
They choke me,—I cannot eat;—no, no, I cannot!
Oh, horrible toil I born of Need and of Dread.
The sweatshop at mid-day—I'll draw you the picture:
A battlefield bloody; the conflict at rest;
Around and about me the corpses are lying;
The blood cries aloud from the earth's gory breast.
A moment . . . and hark! The loud signal is sounded,
The dead rise again and renewed is the fight . . .
They struggle, these corpses; for strangers, for
    strangers!
They struggle, they fall, and they sink into night.
I gaze on the battle in bitterest anger,
And pain, hellish pain wakes the rebel in me!
The clock—now I hear it aright!—It is crying:
"An end to this bondage! An end there must be!"
It quickens my reason, each feeling within me;

It shows me how precious the moments that fly.
Oh, worthless my life if I longer am silent,
And lost to the world if in silence I die.
The man in me sleeping begins to awaken;
The thing that was slave into slumber has passed:
Now; up with the man in me! Up and be doing!
No misery more! Here is freedom at last!
When sudden: a whistle!—the Boss—an alarum!—
I sink in the slime of the stagnant routine;—
There's tumult, they struggle, oh, lost is my ego;—
I know not, I care not, I am a machine! . . .

DRAWING CONCLUSIONS

1. Taken together, what can we learn from Rosenfeld's poem and the International Harvester brochure about the sources of conflict between workers and employers during the age of industrialization?

1.3 PLATFORM OF THE KNIGHTS OF LABOR (1878)

The Knights of Labor was founded in the city of Philadelphia in 1869. It aspired to unite all workers regardless of skill or occupation. The Knights grew rapidly in the mid 1880s and briefly achieved national prominence before falling into decline. This is their 1878 platform.

GUIDING QUESTIONS:

1. How do the Knights of Labor portray the emerging industrial order?
2. What were the specific goals of the Knights of Labor?
3. How might the activities of the Knights of Labor bring workers into conflict with employers?

KNIGHTS OF LABOR PLATFORM— PREAMBLE AND DECLARATION OF PRINCIPLES OF THE ORDER

The alarming development and aggressiveness of capitalists and corporations, unless checked, will inevitably lead to the pauperization and hopeless degradation of the toiling masses.

It is imperative, if we desire to enjoy the full blessings of life, that a check be placed upon unjust accumulation, and the power for evil of aggregated wealth.

This much desired object can be accomplished only by the united efforts of those who obey the divine injunction, "In the sweat of thy face shalt thou eat bread."

Therefore, we have formed the Order of Knights of Labor, for the purpose of organizing and directing the power of the industrial masses, not as a political party, for it is more—in it are crystalized sentiments and measures for the whole people, but it should be borne in mind, when exercising the right of suffrage, that most of the objects herein set forth can only be obtained through legislation, and that it is the duty of all to assist in nominating and supporting with their votes only such candidates as will pledge their support to those measures, regardless of party. But no one shall be compelled to vote with the majority, and calling upon all who believe in securing "the greatest good to the greatest number," to join and assist us, we declare to the world that our aims are:

I. To make industrial and moral worth, not wealth, the true standard of individual and National greatness.

II. To secure to the workers the full enjoyment of the wealth they create, sufficient leisure in which to develop their intellectual, moral and social faculties: all of the benefits, recreation and pleasures of association; in a word, to enable them to share in the gains and honors of advancing civilization.

In order to secure these results, we demand at the hands of the State:

III. The establishment of Bureaus of Labor Statistics, that we may arrive at a correct knowledge of the educational, moral and financial condition of the laboring masses.

IV. That the public lands, the heritage of the people, be reserved for actual settlers; not another acre for railroads or speculators, and that all lands now held for speculative purposes be taxed to their full value.

From *Labor: Its Rights and Wrongs* (Washington, DC: The Labor Publishing Company, 1886), 29–33.

V. The abrogation of all laws that do not bear equally upon capital and labor, and the removal of unjust technicalities, delays and discriminations in the administration of justice.

VI. The adoption of measures providing for the health and safety of those engaged in mining, manufacturing and building industries, and for indemnification to those engaged therein for injuries received through lack of necessary safeguards.

VII. The recognition, by incorporation of trades unions, orders and such other associations as may be organized by the working masses to improve their condition and protect their rights.

VIII. The enactment of laws to compel corporations to pay employees weekly, in lawful money, for the labor of the preceding week, and giving mechanics and laborers a first lien upon the products of their labor to the extent of their wages.

IX. The abolition of the contract system on National, State and Municipal works.

X. The enactment of laws providing for arbitration between employers and employed, and to enforce the decision of the arbitrators.

XI. The prohibition by law of the employment of children under 15 years of age in workshops, mines and factories.

XII. To prohibit the hiring out of convict labor.

XIII. That a graduated income tax be levied.

And we demand at the hands of Congress:

XIV. The establishment of a National monetary system, in which a circulating medium in necessary quantity shall issue direct to the people, without the intervention of banks; that all the National issue shall be full legal tender in payment of all debts, public and private; and that the Government shall not guarantee or recognize any private bank, or create any banking corporations.

XV. That interest-bearing bonds, bills of credit or notes shall never be issued by the Government, but that, when need arises, the emergencies shall be met by issue of legal tender, non-interest-bearing money.

XVI. That the importation of foreign labor under contract be prohibited.

XVII. That in connection with the post-office, the Government shall organize financial exchanges, safe deposits and facilities for deposit of the savings of the people in small sums.

XVIII. That the government shall obtain possession, by purchase, under the right of eminent domain, of all telegraphs, telephones and railroads, and that hereafter no charter or license be issued to any corporation for construction or operation of any means of transporting intelligence, passengers or freight.

And while making the foregoing demands upon the State and National Government, we will endeavor to associate our own labors.

XIX. To establish co-operative institutions such as will tend to supersede the wage-system, by the introduction of a co-operative industrial system.

XX. To secure for both sexes equal pay for equal work.

XXI. To shorten the hours of labor by a general refusal to work for more than eight hours.

XXII. To persuade employers to agree to arbitrate all differences which may arise between them and their employees, in order that the bonds of sympathy between them may be strengthened and that strikes may be rendered unnecessary.

DRAWING CONCLUSIONS

1. What does the Knights of Labor Platform suggest about the concerns of workers during the age of industrialization?
2. What can we learn from this document about the sources of conflict between workers and employers during the age of industrialization?

1.5 SAMUEL GOMPERS ON THE ISSUE OF STRIKES (1899)

Samuel Gompers was a cigar maker who went on to become the most prominent labor leader in the United States. Gompers served over thirty years as president of the American Federation of Labor (AF of L), a national association of trade unions that represented workers primarily in the skilled crafts. In this 1899 testimony before a Congressional commission investigating the relations of labor and capital, Gompers argues for the value and the necessity of both unions and of the strike. Much of his testimony focuses on the issue of union "defense funds." A defense fund allowed a union to sustain a strike for an extended period of time by providing striking workers with payments from the union during the period that they were out of work. Union members paid for the defense fund through their union dues.

GUIDING QUESTIONS:

1. Why does Gompers believe that unions are a necessity of the industrial age?
2. Why does Gompers believe that it is necessary for workers to sometimes engage in strikes?

Q. You would not care now to express an opinion as to the merits of a large defense fund in any organization?

A. Yes: I have no hesitancy at all in expressing an opinion.

Q. The commission would like to hear from you on that.

A. So long as men will have adverse interests, and one side either proposes to fight to defend its interests, or is in a position to fight to defend or further its interests, it is humane, it is just, and it is necessary that the other side also prepare itself to defend or protect or advance its interest. If it does not, it will be annihilated. The defense fund in the hands of the organizations of labor is the material weapon by which the working people can, do, and must protect themselves. Wealth in the hands of the employer is in itself a great power to take advantage of the wage earner, unless the wage earner is organized and in a position to protect himself. There was a time when the individual workingman, when leaving his employment, was somewhat nearer upon an equality in power with the individual employer. Organization then may not have been as essential to the protection of the laborers' interest as it is to-day. To-day the successful employer is that one who employs a very large number of workingmen, and if fair consideration for the employees' rights is to be had at all, the entire number of the employees must act as one man in order to be upon an equality of power and strength, to resist encroachments upon the workers' rights, and be as comparatively strong as the individual workingman was to the individual employer say half a century ago, when the man employing five men was a fairly extensive employer. The acting together, the aggregation, is the unit. The union is the machine by which the best results are to be obtained. It is the discipline of elements that go to make up the army of labor, and a defense fund is the arms and ammunition.

From US Congress, House of Representatives, *Report of the Industrial Commission on the Relations and Conditions of Capital and Labor*, 56th Cong., 2d Sess., *House Document* 495, Pt. 7, 598–608.

I believe in the defense fund, that employers may understand in the beginning that they can not trivially or lightly attempt to reduce wages; that they can not enforce obnoxious conditions, say for the increasing number of hours of labor, obnoxious shop rules, unsanitary conditions of employment, surroundings, etc.; that they cannot lightly or inconsiderately do these things with knowing beforehand that the workers are organized and are in a position to withstand for a considerable time any attempt on the part of the employer to enforce these conditions which the organized employees would resent. On the other hand a large fund, a defense fund being part of it, is the better fund than any. A large fund in the organization is the preventive of the reduction of wages during dull times, and it gives the better opportunity to workingmen to obtain concessions when industry revives. We have seen that when organizations have had little or no funds and an industrial crisis comes, as it does under our economic conditions, periodically—there is a periodicity about out industrial crises that is very noticeable to the student—when these years of industrial stagnation come upon us and the workers are only partly organized and have little funds, they are the easiest to succumb to the constant reductions in their wages; and when an industrial revival takes place they are the last to receive any of its benefits. It is the organizations of the working people which are best prepared to withstand injustice or reductions in wages that succeed best in resistance. They maintain the organization during periods of depression are already in position to take advantage of the better opportunities which present themselves by reason of a revival of industry, while on the other hand, those who have suffered most lose a very large part of their organization, if not entirely, and much of the time is lost in the effort to bring the men together to reorganize. "There is a tide in the affairs of men, which, if taken at the flood," etc.

Q: What do you say of the proposition, accepted, as I understand, by trades unions usually, that the larger the defense fund and the higher the dues of any union, the stronger they are and the more sure they are to protect their rights?

A. That proposition can not be successfully disputed; and, too, the large fund in an organization is the greatest contributing cause to a diminution in the number of strikes.

Q: Would you care to mention the position of the cigar makers' union in respect to the fund and the strike matter?

A. The Cigar Makers' International Union, of which I have the honor of being a member, and have been since 1864, continuously, was at one time an incoherent mass of federated members into a federated number of local unions, each absolutely independent of the other, except that they could, if they chose, accept a member's traveling card and accord him the hand of fellowship. During the early history of the organization it possessed no real merit, until a strike occurred and brought about an understanding among my fellow-craftsmen that there was something more necessary than simply the declaration that one was a union man, and that was that wherever you are a union man, you are naturally to observe the same obligations, perform the same duties, and be entitled to the same privileges and benefits. That dawned upon us just after a great strike and just previous to the greater strike of 1877, when there were about 10,000 cigar makers out on strike, after suffering all the miseries that one could imagine. It was at the convention of 1877 that we adopted the first proposition of uniform dues and uniform initiation fees. Previous to that one local union would charge $5 for initiation fee, another one would charge $3, another, not so fortunately situated, would charge 10 cents, or, perhaps accept them without any initiation fee at all, and usually where we charged very low figures they used to run in swarms. If I could coin a word expressive of the way they ran out, I should be glad to—the way they left the organization. And this was true, too, of the lack of uniformity in dues; lack of uniformity of duties and rights. We gradually introduced a system by which not only the dues were increased, but the funds belonged to the membership in their collective capacity, but were held in the local unions, never at general headquarters. We established a system, too, by which a member was entitled to the same benefits—strike benefit, lockout benefit, victimization benefit, sick benefit, traveling benefit—that is, when a member was out of employment, so that he need not be arrested as a tramp or vagrant his union card entitled him to a loan from the union under whose jurisdiction he was, so that he could travel to the next point, and get 50 cents in addition to the mileage, so as to buy a meal or get a lodging, and from place to place those loans were accorded to him until he could return to work, and then he paid 10 per cent of his wages in repaying the organization the loan advanced. It was a loan system, without interest, of course. Then there was the out-of-work benefit— benefit when a man is out of work; that condition for which society makes no provision at all, not even the charitably inclined. Our organization proposed to go to the defense of the member and pay him, not a stipend as a matter of charity, but something in his own right as a contributing member. Then the death benefit, from $50 for the first year of a membership to $550 to a member's family or nearest of kin for 15 years' membership. There is a graduated figure or sum between those sums. We pay 30 cents per week as dues for these benefits, and we receive in return a larger amount in the shape of benefits, direct benefits, than is paid by any insurance or beneficial association on earth. The combination makes its administration economical. The percentage of expenditure for administration is very small; and this does not refer to the strike benefit or lockout benefit, or victimization benefit.

During the early history of our organization the men would be on a strike at least, I should say, 2 months of the year. Cigar makers were continually on strike, very much like the coal miners were between 1893 and 1897—always striking. At any rate they had not lost their manhood and courage to protest against wrong. They were going down during those years, but they were fighting all the time, and the fighting quality came to their relief when they entered into their great contest in 1897, which brought about, I might say, the last of the great misery of the miners. A transformation took place in our trade. Our constant fighting at least maintained within us some grit to protest at some opportune time to advantage. In the early history of

the organization we expended hundreds of thousands of dollars on strikes. The greater proportion of our funds was expended in strikes. I could give you the figures, but not just now. Mr. Perkins, the president of that organization, I think it would be better if he should give that testimony. I would not care to intrench upon the ground that he ought probably to cover. I would say that in the same proportion that we increased our dues from 10 cents per week to 30 we had less strikes, consequently less expenditure for strikes, and, notwithstanding that, our strikes in the later years were usually of a character for improvement, for the higher wage. There were very few strikes during the industrial depression between 1893 and 1897. There were very few great strikes in which our trade was involved by reason of the fact—that we attributed, rather—that the organization was numerically and financially strong and could resist for a very long period any attempt on the part of the employers to reduce wages. Their experience had taught them that a fight with the cigar makers was expensive at any time, and that with the organization and its large treasury it might be interminable. In 1883, when we were only paying 15 cents per week dues, a strike of cigar makers in Cincinnati, involving about 1,800 people, lasted for 13 months. We did not win the strike, but the employers do not exist in Cincinnati. The trade went elsewhere, and where that trade went the cigar makers went and higher wages went; and though the strike was lost in Cincinnati, as an effect of the strike the good result was obtained.

. . .

Q. (By Mr. C. J. Harris.) "Economic results of strikes and of lockouts." You might take the subject as a whole.

A. The strikes, I should say, might be defined as a suspension of labor for the purpose of discussing and arriving at terms under which industry or commerce, or both, can be resumed; and the cause of a strike is the dissatisfaction on the part of employees with the terms under which production or distribution, or both, have been carried on. A lockout is the aggressive action on the part of employers, with the same purposes in view. The working people find that improvements in the methods of production and distribution are constantly being made, and unless they occasionally strike, or have the power to enter upon a strike, the improvements will all go to the employer and all the injuries to the employees. A strike is an effort on the part of the workers to obtain some of the improvements that have occurred resultant from bygone and present genius of our intelligence, of our mental progress. We are producing wealth to-day at a greater ratio than ever in the history of mankind, and a strike on the part of workers is, first, against deterioration in their condition, and, second, to be participants in some of the improvements. Strikes are caused from various reasons. The employer desires to reduce wages and lengthen hours of labor, while the desire on the part of employees is to obtain shorter hours of labor and better wages, and better surroundings. Strikes establish or maintain the rights of unionism; that is, to establish and maintain the organization by which the rights of the workers can be the better protected and advanced against the little forms of oppression, sometimes economical, sometimes political—the effort on the part of employers to influence and intimidate workmen's political preferences; strikes against victimization; activity in the cause of the workers against the blacklist. I had the pleasure of hearing the testimony given by Mr. Clark, the grand chief of the Order of Railway Conductors, upon the question of the blacklist, and 1 heard the question propounded by one of the members of the commission as to letters of recommendation that have certain watermarks on the paper, or printed or written upon any particular tint of paper, and he said that itself oftentimes would be enough warning to employers when this letter of recommendation was presented. Men who have been for long years with the trade unions have termed these letters of recommendation to be nothing more or less than a "ticket of leave," such as was presented often in the olden times by the convict as evidence of good character, at once establishing the fact that he was a convict, and that he was not required under the old rule in penology to present this ticket of leave upon his own merits, upon his own determination to be honest and live an honest life ever after.

There have been a number of trades that have gone on strikes and suffered a long time for the abolition of what they then termed a ticket of leave, and I trust that the time is not far distant when the railway men will have power enough to abolish that system of presenting letters of recommendation to companies of which they want employment.

. . .

Q. (By Mr. Farquhar.) What is the result in the last 10 years? Have strikes decreased or increased—that is, compared with the increase of organized labor?

A. During the first year of organizations, as a rule, there are strikes. When workmen remain organized for any considerable length of time, strikes are reduced in number. It is a peculiar fact that when workmen are unorganized they imagine their employers are almighty and themselves absolutely impotent. When workmen organize for the first time, this transformation takes place: they imagine their employers absolutely impotent and themselves almighty, and the result of it is there is conflict. The employer, so far as strikes begun in his establishment are concerned, resents immediately the assumption of the workmen to appear by committee. He has been accustomed to look upon himself, as to his factory or his establishment, as "monarch of all he surveys" with undisputed sway, and the fact that his employees have an entity as an organization, to be represented by a committee, is something unheard of by him and absolutely intolerable. He imagines immediately that it is a question as to his right to his property; imagines immediately that his property is threatened, and surrounds himself with such safeguards—as the lamented Gladstone once said, "The entire resources of civilization had not yet been exhausted"—arms everybody who swears loyalty to the company, and often surrounds himself with a mercenary armed force, and all the wiles and devices that the acumen of our legal friends can suggest are always employed to overcome, overawe these "mutineers" against his authority.

Q. (By Mr. Ratchford.) To what extent, if any, is the employer, in your judgment, responsible for that condition of affairs?

A. To the same extent that the bourgeois of France, the royalists of France, were responsible in cowing the people of France, which resulted in the revolution and the brutality manifested by the people when they got power. The employers have simply cut wages whenever they thought it convenient. They looked upon their employees as part of the machinery; to exhibit, perhaps, some little sympathy when one was very critically injured or suffering, and then expected the worship of them all; the cutting of wages time and again, in season and out of season; the discharge of a man who proposed to exercise his right as a man, whether it was as a workman or as a citizen; and so on, driving practically the courage and heart out of the man; and when, through some incident, of which there are thousands, the men are organized of their own volition, quite frequently they touch shoulders for the first time outside of the shop—they touch shoulders, and the thrill simply enthuses them and intoxicates them with new-found power. It is only after the organization has administered a very costly lesson to the employer, and it is only after the workmen themselves have felt the pangs of hunger, perhaps, or other sacrifices resultant from strikes they suffer when unprepared, unorganized, that they are more careful of each other—both sides. They organize and try to meet each other and discuss with each other, and the better the workmen are organized the more able are they to convince the employer that there is an ethical side to the demands of labor. It required 40,000 people in the city of New York in my own trade in 1877 to demonstrate to the employers that we had a right to be heard in our own defense of our trade, and an opportunity to be heard in our own interests. It cost the miners of the country, in 1897, 16 weeks of suffering to secure a national conference and a national agreement. It cost the railroad brotherhoods long months of suffering, many of them sacrificing their positions, in the railroad strike of 1877, and in the Chicago, Burlington and Quincy strike, of the same year, to secure from the employers the right to be heard through committees, their representatives—that is, their committees of the organization to secure these rights. Workmen have had to stand the brunt of the suffering. The American Republic was not established without some suffering, without some sacrifice, and no tangible right has yet been achieved in the interest of the people unless it has been secured by sacrifices and persistency. After a while we become a little more tolerant to each other and recognize all have rights; get around the table and chaff each other; all recognize that they were not so reasonable in the beginning. Now we propose to meet and discuss our interests, and if we can not agree we propose in a more reasonable way to conduct our contests, each to decide how to hold out and bring the other one to terms. A strike, too, is to industry as the right that the British people contended for in placing in the House of Commons the power to close the purse strings to the Government. The rights of the British people were secured in two centuries—between 1500 and 1600—more than ever before, by the securing of that power to withhold the supplies; tied up the purse strings and compelled the Crown to yield. A strike on the part of workmen is to close production and compel better terms and more rights to be acceded to the producers. The economic results of strikes to workers have been advantageous. Without strikes their rights would not have been considered. It is not that workmen or organized labor desires the strike, but it will tenaciously hold to the right to strike. We recognize that peaceful industry is necessary to successful civilized life, but the right to strike and the preparation to strike is the greatest preventive to strikes. If the workmen were to make up their minds to-morrow that they would under no circumstances strike, the employers would do all the striking for them in the way of lesser wages and longer hours of labor.

DRAWING CONCLUSIONS:

1. What can we learn from this document about the sources of conflict between workers and employers during the age of industrialization?

1.6 ANDREW CARNEGIE, "AN EMPLOYER'S VIEW OF THE LABOR QUESTION" (1886)

Born into a working-class Scottish immigrant family, by the late nineteenth century Andrew Carnegie was one of the country's leading industrialists and one of its wealthiest individuals. In the 1870s, he introduced the Bessemer process for the mass production of steel to the United States; and from this foundation, he built the Carnegie Steel Company into an industrial giant. In this 1886 piece, Carnegie shares his views on the issue of labor relations. He expresses sympathy for the plight of working people. Nonetheless, just six years later, he and the Carnegie Steel Company found themselves locked in a violent confrontation with striking workers at its Homestead Steel Works. As you read Carnegie's views, ask yourself what likely brought he and his company into conflict with organized labor.

GUIDING QUESTIONS:

1. What is Carnegie's view of unions?
2. What does Carnegie think is the cause of strikes?
3. How does Carnegie propose to prevent strikes?

AN EMPLOYER'S VIEW OF THE LABOR QUESTION ANDREW CARNEGIE

The struggle in which labor has been engaged during the past three hundred years, first against authority and then against capital, has been a triumphal march. Victory after victory has been achieved. Even so late as in Shakespeare's time, remains of villein age or serfdom still existed in England. Before that not only the labor but the person of the laborer belonged to the chief. The workers were either slaves or serfs; men and women were sold with the estate upon which they worked, and became the property of the new lord, just as did the timber which grew on the land. In those days we hear nothing of strikes or of trades-unions, or differences of opinion between employer and employed. The fact is, labor had then no right which the chief, or employer, was bound to respect. Even as late as the beginning of this century, the position of the laborer in some departments was such as can scarcely be credited. What do our laboring friends think of this, that down to 1779 the miners of Britain were in a state of serfdom. They "were compelled by law to remain in the pits as long as the owner chose to keep them at work there, and were actually sold as part of the capital invested in the works. If they accepted an engagement elsewhere, their master could always have them fetched back and flogged as thieves for having attempted to rob him of their labor. This law was modified in 1779, but was not repealed till after the acts passed in 1797 and 1799" (The Trades-Unions of England, p. 119). This was only ninety-seven years ago. Men are still living who were living then. Again, in France, as late as 1806, every workman had to procure a license; and in Russia, down to our own days, agricultural laborers were sold with the soil they tilled.

Consider the change, nay, the revolution. Now the poorest laborer in America or in England, or indeed throughout the civilized world, who can handle a pick or a shovel, stands upon equal terms with the purchaser of his labor. He sells or withholds it as may seem best to him. He negotiates, and thus rises to the dignity

From *Labor: Its Rights and Wrongs* (Washington, DC: The Labor Publishing Company, 1886), 89–105.

of an independent contractor. When he has performed the work he bargained to do, he owes his employer nothing, and is under no obligation to him. Not only has the laborer conquered his political and personal freedom: he has achieved industrial freedom as well, as far as the law can give it, and he now fronts his master, proclaiming himself his equal under the law.

But, notwithstanding this complete revolution, it is evident that the permanent relations to each other of labor and capital have not yet evolved. The present adjustment does not work without friction, and changes must be made before we can have industrial peace. To-day we find collisions between these forces, capital and labor, when there should be combination. The mill hands of an industrial village in France have just risen against their employers, attacked the manager's home and killed him. The streets of another French village are barricaded against the expected forces of order. The ship-builders of Sunderland, in England, are at the verge of starvation, owing to a quarrel with their employers; and Leicester has just been the scene of industrial riots. In our country, labor disputes and strikes were never so numerous as now. East and West, North and South, everywhere, there is unrest, showing that an equilibrium has not yet been reached between employers and employed.

A strike or lockout is, in itself, a ridiculous affair. Whether a failure or a success, it gives no direct proof of its justice or injustice. In this it resembles war between two nations. It is simply a question of strength and endurance between the contestants. The gage of battle, or the duel, is not more senseless, as a means of establishing what is just and fair, than an industrial strike or lockout. It would be folly to conclude that we have reached any permanent adjustment between capital and labor until strikes and lockouts are as much things of the past as the gage of battle or the duel have become in the most advanced communities.

Taking for granted, then, that some further modifications must be made between capital and labor, I propose to consider the various plans that have been suggested by which labor can advance another stage in its development in relation to capital. And, as a preliminary, let it be noted that it is only labor and capital in their greatest masses which it is necessary to consider. It is only in large establishments that the industrial

unrest of which I have spoken ominously manifests itself. The farmer who hires a man to assist him, or the gentleman who engages a groom or a butler, is not affected by strikes. The innumerable cases in which a few men only are directly concerned, which comprise in the aggregate the most of labor, present upon the whole a tolerably satisfactory condition of affairs. This clears the ground of much, and leaves us to deal only with the immense mining and manufacturing concerns of recent growth, in which capital and labor often array themselves in alarming antagonism.

Among expedients suggested for their better reconciliation, the first place must be assigned to the idea of cooperation, or the plan by which the workers are to become part-owners in enterprises, and share their fortunes. There is no doubt that if this could be effected it would have the same beneficial effect upon the workman which the ownership of land has upon the man who has hitherto tilled the land for another. The sense of ownership would make of him more of a man as regards himself, and hence more of a citizen as regards the commonwealth. But we are here met by a difficulty which I confess I have not yet been able to overcome, and which renders me less sanguine than I should like to be in regard to cooperation. The difficulty is this, and it seems to me inherent in all gigantic manufacturing, mining, and commercial operations. Two men or two combinations of men will erect blast-furnaces, iron-mills, cotton-mills, or piano manufactories adjoining each other, or engage in shipping or commercial business. They will start with actual capital and credit; and to those only superficially acquainted with the *personnel* of these concerns, success will seem as likely to attend the one as the other. Nevertheless, one will fail after dragging along a lifeless existence, and pass into the hands of its creditors; while the neighboring mill or business will make a fortune for its owners. Now, the successful manufacturer, dividing every month or every year a proportion of his profits among his workmen, either as a bonus or as dividends upon shares owned by them, will not only have a happy and contented body of operatives, but he will inevitably attract from his rival the very best workmen in every department. His rival, having no profits to divide among his workmen, and paying them only a small assured minimum to enable them to live, finds himself despoiled of foremen and of workmen necessary to carry on his business successfully. His workmen are discontented and, in their own opinion, defrauded of the proper fruits of their skill, through incapacity or inattention of their employers. Thus, unequal business capacity in the management produces unequal results. It will be precisely the same if one of these manufactories belongs to the workmen themselves; but in this case, in the present stage of development of the workmen, the chances of failure will be enormously increased. It is, indeed, greatly to be doubted whether any body of working-men in the world could to-day organize and successfully carry on a mining or manufacturing or commercial business in competition with concerns owned by men trained to affairs. If any such cooperative organization succeeds, it may be taken for granted that it is principally owing to the exceptional business ability of one of the managers, and only in a very small degree to the efforts of the mass of workmen-owners. This business ability is excessively rare, as is proved by the incredibly large proportion of those who enter upon the stormy sea of business only to fail. I should say that twenty cooperative concerns would fail to every one that would succeed. There are, of course, a few successful establishments, notably two in France and one in England, which are organized upon the cooperative plan, in which the workmen participate in the profits. But these were all created by the present owners, who now generously share the profits with their workmen, and are making the success of their manufactories upon the cooperative plan the proud work of their lives. What these concerns will become when the genius for affairs is no longer with them to guide, is a matter of grave doubt and, to me, of foreboding. I can, of course, picture in my mind a state of civilization in which the most talented business men shall find their most cherished work in carrying on immense concerns, not primarily for their own personal aggrandizement, but for the good of the masses of workers engaged therein, and their families; but this is only a foreshadowing of a dim and distant future. When a class of such men has evolved, the problem of capital and labor will be permanently solved to the entire satisfaction of both. But as this

manifestly belongs to a future generation, I cannot consider cooperation, or common ownership, as the next immediate step in advance which it is possible for labor to make in its path upward.

The next suggestion is that peaceful settlement of differences should be reached through arbitration. Here we are upon firmer ground. I would lay it down as a maxim that there is no excuse for a strike or a lockout until arbitration of differences has been offered by one party and refused by the other. No doubt serious trouble attends even arbitration at present, from the difficulty of procuring suitable men to judge intelligently between the disputants. There is a natural disinclination among business men to expose their business to men in whom they have not entire confidence. We lack so far in America a retired class of men of affairs. Our vile practice is to keep on accumulating more dollars until we die. If it were the custom here, as it is in England, for men to withdraw from active business after acquiring a fortune, this class would furnish the proper arbitrators. On the other hand, the ex-presidents of trades-unions, such as Mr. Jarrett or Mr. Wihle, after they have retired from active control, would commend themselves to the manufacturers and to the men as possessed of the necessary technical knowledge, and educated to a point where commercial reasons would not be without their proper weight upon them. I consider that of all the agencies immediately available to prevent wasteful and embittering contests between capital and labor, arbitration is the most powerful and most beneficial.

The influence of trades-unions upon the relations between the employer and employed has been much discussed. Some establishments in America have refused to recognize the right of the men to form themselves into these unions, although I am not aware that any concern in England would dare to take this position.

This policy, however, may be regarded as only a temporary phase of the situation. The right of the working-men to combine and to form trades unions is no less sacred than the right of the manufacturer to enter into associations and conferences with his fellows, and it must sooner or later be conceded. Indeed, it gives one but a poor opinion of the American workman if he permits himself to be deprived of a right which his fellow in England long since conquered for himself. My experience has been that trades-unions, upon the whole, are beneficial both to labor and to capital. They certainly educate the working-men, and give them a truer conception of the relations of capital and labor than they could otherwise form. The ablest and best workmen eventually come to the front in these organizations; and it may be laid down as a rule that the more intelligent the workman the fewer the contests with employers. It is not the intelligent workman, who knows that labor without his brother capital is helpless, but the blatant ignorant man, who regards capital as the natural enemy of labor, who does so much to embitter the relations between employer and employed; and the power of this ignorant demagogue arises chiefly from the lack of proper organization among the men through which their real voice can be expressed. This voice will always be found in favor of the judicious and intelligent representative. Of course, as men become intelligent more deference must be paid to them personally and to their rights, and even to their opinions and prejudices; and, upon the whole, a greater share of profits must be paid in the day of prosperity to the intelligent than to the ignorant workman. He cannot be imposed upon so readily. On the other hand, he will be found much readier to accept reduced compensation when business is depressed; and it is better in the long run for capital to be served by the highest intelligence, and to be made well aware of the fact that it is dealing with men who know what is due to them, both as to treatment and compensation.

One great source of the trouble between employers and employed arises from the fact that the immense establishments of to-day, in which alone we find serious conflicts between capital and labor, are not managed by their owners, but by salaried officers, who cannot possibly have any permanent interest in the welfare of the working-men. These officials are chiefly anxious to present a satisfactory balance-sheet at the end of the year, that their hundreds of shareholders may receive the usual dividends, and that they may therefore be secure in their positions, and be allowed to manage the business without unpleasant interference either by directors or shareholders. It is notable that bitter strikes seldom occur in small establishments where the owner comes into direct contact with his men, and knows their qualities, their struggles, and their aspirations. It is the chairman, situated hundreds of miles away from his men, who only pays a flying visit to the works and perhaps finds time to walk through the mill or mine once or twice a year, that is chiefly responsible for the disputes which break out at intervals. I have noticed that the manager who confers oftenest with a committee of his leading men has the least trouble with his workmen. Although it may be impracticable for the presidents of these large corporations to know the working-men personally, the manager at the mills, having a committee of his best men to present their suggestions and wishes from time to time, can do much to maintain and strengthen amicable relations, if not interfered with from headquarters. I, therefore, recognize in trades-unions, or, better still, in organizations of the men of each establishment, who select representatives to speak for them, a means, not of further embittering the relations between employer and employed, but of improving them.

It is astonishing how small a sacrifice upon the part of the employer will sometimes greatly benefit the men. I remember that at one of our meetings with a committee, it was incidentally remarked by one speaker that the necessity for obtaining credit at the stores in the neighborhood was a grave tax upon the men. An ordinary workman, he said, could not afford to maintain himself and family for a month, and as he only received his pay monthly, he was compelled to obtain credit and to pay exorbitantly for everything, whereas, if he had the cash, he could buy at twenty-five per cent less. "Well," I said, "why cannot we overcome that by paying every two weeks?" The reply was: "We did not like to ask it, because we have always understood that it would cause much trouble; but if you do that it will be worth an advance of five per cent in our wages." We have paid semi-monthly since. Another speaker happened to say that although they were in the midst of coal, the price charged for small lots delivered at their houses was a certain sum per bushel. The price named was double what our best coal was costing us. How easy for us to deliver to our men such coal as they required, and charge them cost! This was done without a cent's loss to us, but with much gain to the men.

Several other points similar to these have arisen by which their labors might be lightened or products increased, and others suggesting changes in machinery or facilities which, but for the conferences referred to, would have been unthought of by the employer and probably never asked for by the men. For these and other reasons I attribute the greatest importance to an organization of the men, through whose duly elected representatives the managers may be kept informed from time to time of their grievances and suggestions. No matter how able the manager, the clever workman can often show him how beneficial changes can be made in the special branch in which that workman labors. Unless the relations between manager and workmen are not only amicable but friendly, the owners miss much; nor is any man a first-class manager who has not the confidence and respect, and even the admiration, of his workmen. No man is a true gentleman who does not inspire the affection and devotion of his servants. The danger is that such committees may ask conferences too often; three or four meetings per year should be regarded as sufficient.

I come now to the greatest cause of the friction which prevails between capital and labor in the largest establishments the real essence of the trouble, and the remedy I have to propose.

The trouble is that the men are not paid at any time the compensation proper to that time. All large concerns necessarily keep filled with orders, say for six months in advance, and these orders are taken, of course, at prices prevailing when they are booked. This year's operations furnish perhaps the best illustration of the difficulty. Steel rails at the end of last year for delivery this year were $29 per ton at the works. Of course the mills entered orders freely at this price, and kept on entering them until the demand growing unexpectedly great carried prices up to $35 per ton. Now, the various mills in America are compelled for the next six months or more to run up orders which do not average $31 per ton at the seaboard and Pittsburg and pay $34 at Chicago. Transportation, ironstone, and prices of all kinds have advanced upon them in the meantime, and they must therefore run the bulk of the year upon very small margins of profit. But the men, noticing in the papers the "great boom in steel rails," very naturally demand their share of the advance, and, under existing faulty arrangements between capital and labor, they have secured it. The employers, therefore, have grudgingly given what they know under proper arrangements they should not have been required to give, and there has been friction, and still is dissatisfaction upon the part of the employers. Reverse this picture. The steel-rail market falls again. The mills have still six months' work at prices above the prevailing market, and can afford to pay men higher wages than the then existing state of the market would apparently justify. But having just been amerced in extra payments for labor which they should not have paid, they naturally attempt to reduce wages as the market price of rails goes down, and there arises discontent among the men, and we have a repetition of the negotiations and strikes which have characterized the beginning of this year. In other words, when the employer is going down the employee insists on going up, and *vice versa*. What we must seek is a plan by which the men will receive high wages when their employers are receiving high prices for their product, and hence are making large profits; and, per contra, when the employers are receiving low prices for product, and therefore small if any profits, the men will receive low wages. If this plan can be found, employers and employed will be "in the same boat," rejoicing together in their prosperity, and calling into play their fortitude together in adversity. There will be no room for quarrels, and instead of a feeling of antagonism there will be a feeling of partnership between employers and employed.

There is a simple means of producing this result, and to its general introduction both employers and employed should steadily bend their energies. Wages should be based upon a sliding scale, in proportion to the net prices received for product month by month. And I here gladly pay Mr. Potter, president of the North Chicago Rolling Mill Company, the great compliment to say that he has already taken a step in this direction, for to-day he is working his principal mill upon this plan. The result is that he has had no stoppage whatever this year, nor any dissatisfaction. All has gone smoothly along, and this in itself is worth at least as much to the manufacturer and to the men as the difference in wages one way or another which can arise from the new system.

The celebrated Crescent Steel Works of Pittsburg, manufacturers of the highest grades of tool steel, pay their skilled workmen by a sliding scale, based upon prices received for product—an important factor in the eminent success of that firm. The scale adopted by the iron manufacturers and workmen is only an approach to the true sliding scale; nevertheless it is a decided gain both to capital and labor, as it is adopted from year to year, and hence eliminates strikes on account of wages during the year, and limits these interruptions from that cause to the yearly negotiation as to the justice or injustice of the scale. As this scale, however, is not based upon the prices actually received for product, but upon the published list of prices, which should be received in theory, there is not complete mutuality between the parties. In depressed times, such as the iron industry has been passing through in recent years, enormous concessions upon the published card prices have been necessary to effect sales, and in these the workmen have not shared with their employers. If, however, there was added to the scale, even in its present form, a stipulation that all causes of difference which could not be postponed till the end of the year, and then considered with the scale, should be referred to arbitration, and that, in case of failure of the owners and workmen to agree at the yearly conference, arbitration should also be resorted to, strikes and lockouts would be entirely eliminated from the iron business; and if the award of the arbitrators took effect from the date of reference the works could run without a day's interruption.

Dismissing, therefore, for the present all consideration of cooperation as not being within measurable distance, I believe that the next steps in the advance toward permanent, peaceful relations between capital and labor are:

First: That compensation be paid the men based upon a sliding scale in proportion to the prices received for product.

Second: A proper organization of the men of every works to be made, by which the natural leaders, the best men, will eventually come to the front and confer freely with the employers.

Third: Peaceful arbitration to be in all cases resorted to for the settlement of differences which the owners and the mill committee cannot themselves adjust in friendly conference.

Fourth: No interruption ever to occur to the operations of the establishment, since the decision of the arbitrators shall be made to take effect from the date of reference.

If these measures were adopted by an establishment, several important advantages would be gained:

First: The employer and employed would simultaneously share their prosperity or adversity with each other. The scale once settled, the feeling of antagonism would be gone, and a feeling of mutuality would ensue. Capital and labor would be shoulder to shoulder, supporting each other.

Second: There could be neither strike nor lockout, since both parties had agreed to abide by a forthcoming decision of disputed points. Knowing that in the last resort strangers were to be called in to decide what should be a family affair, the cases would, indeed, be few which would not be amicably adjusted by the original parties without calling in others to judge between them.

Whatever the future may have in store for labor, the evolutionist, who sees nothing but certain and steady progress for the race, will never attempt to set bounds to its triumphs, even to its final form of complete and universal industrial cooperation, which I hope is some day to be reached. But I am persuaded that the next step forward is to be in the direction I have here ventured to point out; and as one who is now most anxious to contribute his part toward helping forward the day of amicable relations between the two forces of capital and labor, which are not enemies, but are really auxiliaries who stand or fall together, I ask at the hands of both capital and labor a careful consideration of these views.

DRAWING CONCLUSIONS:

1. How is Carnegie's view of labor relations and unions similar to or different from that of Samuel Gompers?

2. Taken together, what can we learn from the Gompers and Carnegie documents about the sources of conflict between workers and employers during the age of industrialization?

1.7 UNITED STATES V. WORKINGMEN'S AMALGAMATED COUNCIL OF NEW ORLEANS, ET AL. (1893)

Among the greatest obstacles the labor movement faced in the late nineteenth century was hostility from many government officials, from the local to the national level. Particularly damaging were a series of state and federal court rulings that found certain trade union practices to be illegal. *United States v. Workingmen's Amalgamated Council of New Orleans* was one such decision. In this 1893 ruling, a federal court found that certain forms of strike activity were in violation of the Sherman Antitrust Act, an 1890 law designed to prevent large companies and corporations from engaging in activities that undermined free economic competition.

The court ruling grew out of an 1892 city-wide general strike in New Orleans called when the city's merchants refused to recognize and negotiate with unions that represented their employees. In response, the trade unions in a range of industries withheld their labor and brought commerce in the city to a standstill. The following year, a federal court found that this concerted strike activity constituted an illegal restraint on trade and was thus a violation of federal law.

GUIDING QUESTIONS:

1. What was the court's reasoning for declaring the New Orleans general strike to be illegal?
2. What impact would a court decision like this have on unions and their ability to operate?

UNITED STATES V. WORKINGMEN'S AMALGAMATED COUNCIL OF NEW ORLEANS ET AL.

Circuit Court, Eastern District Louisiana
54 F. 994; 1893 U.S. App.
March 25, 1893
Opinion by District Judge Edward Coke Billings

This cause is submitted upon an application for an injunction on the bill of complaint, answer, and numerous affidavits and exhibits. The bill of complaint in this case is filed by the United States under the act of congress entitled "An act to protect trade and commerce against unlawful restraint and monopolies." The substance of the bill is that there is a gigantic and widespread combination of the members of a multitude of separate organizations for the purpose of restraining the commerce among the several states and with foreign countries. It avers that a disagreement between the warehousemen and their employees and the principal draymen and their subordinates had been adopted by all the organizations named in the bill, until, by this vast combination of men and of organizations, it was threatened that, unless there was an acquiescence in the demands of the subordinate workmen and draymen, all the men in all of the defendant organizations would leave work, and would allow no work in any department of business; that violence was threatened and used in support of this demand; and that this demand included the interstate and foreign commerce which flows through the city of New Orleans. The bill further states that the proceedings on the part of the defendants had taken such a vast and ramified proportion that, in consequence of the threats of the defendants, the whole business of the city of New Orleans was paralyzed, and the transit of goods and merchandise which was being conveyed through it from state to state, and to and from foreign countries, was totally interrupted. . . .

A difference had sprung up between the warehousemen and their employees and the principal draymen and their subordinates. With the view and purpose to compel an acquiescence on the part of the employers in the demands of the employed, it was finally brought about by the employed that all the union men—that is, all the members of the various labor associations—were made by their officers, clothed with authority under the various charters, to discontinue business, and one of these kinds of business was transporting goods which were being conveyed from state to state, and to and from foreign countries. In some branches of business the effort was made to replace the union men by other workmen. This was resisted by the intimidation springing from vast throngs of the union men assembling in the streets, and in some instances by violence; so that the result was that, by the intended effects of the doings of these defendants, not a bale of goods constituting the commerce of the country could be moved. The question simply is, do these facts establish a case within the statute? It seems to me this question is tantamount to the question, could there be a case under the statute? It is conceded that the labor organizations were at the outset lawful. But, when lawful forces are put into unlawful channels,—i.e. when lawful associations adopt and further unlawful purposes and do unlawful acts,—the associations themselves become unlawful. The evil, as well as the unlawfulness, of the act of the defendants, consists in this: that, until certain demands of theirs were complied with, they endeavored to prevent, and did prevent, everybody from moving the commerce of the country. What is meant by "restraint of trade" is well defined by Chief Justice Savage in People v. Fisher, 14 Wend. 18. He says:

> "The mechanic is not obliged by law to labor for any particular price. He may say that he will not make coarse boots for less than one dollar per pair; but he has no right to say that no other mechanic shall make them for less. Should the journeymen bakers refuse to work unless for enormous wages, which the master bakers could not afford to pay, and should they compel all journeymen in the city to stop work, the whole population must be without bread; so of journeymen tailors or mechanics of any description. Such combinations would be productive of derangement and confusion, which certainly must be injurious to trade."

It is the successful effort of the combination of the defendants to intimidate and overawe others who were at work in conducting or carrying on the commerce of the country, in which the court finds their error and their violation of the statute. One of the intended results of their combined action was the forced stagnation of all the commerce which flowed through New Orleans. This intent all combined action are none the less unlawful because they included in their scope the paralysis of all other business within the city as well.

DRAWING CONCLUSIONS:

1. What does this document reveal about the restrictions that labor unions faced during the era of industrialization?
2. What can we learn from this document about the sources of conflict between workers and employers during the age of industrialization?

1.8 "THE TRAMPS' TERROR" (1877)

This ad for the Western Gun Works long-range revolver appeared in *Leslie's Illustrated Newspaper* in 1877, toward the end of the painful economic depression of the mid 1870s. As is true today, fear can be a powerful tool in marketing products to the public. As you examine this advertisement, think about how the manufacturer is using fear of social disorder to sell firearms.

GUIDING QUESTIONS:

1. What is the central message of this advertisement to potential firearms purchasers?
2. What does the ad reveal about the attitudes and fears of more prosperous Americans during the age of industrialization?

FIGURE 1. *LESLIE'S ILLUSTRATED NEWSPAPER*, "THE TRAMPS' TERROR" (1877)
Advertisement on page 86 of *Frank Leslie's Weekly*, online database, April 7, 1877 issue: "Our New Model LONG RANGE Revolver Tramps Terror."©

DRAWING CONCLUSIONS:

1. What can we learn from this document about the sources of conflict between workers and employers during the age of industrialization?

PRIMARY SOURCES ON POPULISM

These documents provide insights into the agrarian protests that culminated in the Populist movement of the 1890s. The sources include materials from rank-and-file Populists as well as Populist leaders and from the People's Party itself. A popular song reflecting the grievances of farmers and the recollections of an anti-Populist newspaper editor from Kansas are also included. As you work with these sources, ask yourself what they reveal about the frustrations felt by farmers in the late nineteenth century as well as the factors that led to the widespread agrarian protests of the era.

2.1 THE OMAHA PLATFORM (1892)

In July of 1892, delegates from a variety of farmer, labor, and reform organizations gathered in Omaha, Nebraska, for the first national convention of the People's Party. The platform adopted at the Omaha convention is the clearest and most famous statement of Populist principles.

GUIDING QUESTIONS:

1. How does the Omaha Platform portray the emerging industrial order?
2. What were the specific goals of the People's Party?

THE OMAHA PLATFORM

JULY 4, 1892

NATIONAL PEOPLE'S PARTY PLATFORM

Assembled upon the 116th anniversary of the Declaration of Independence, the People's Party of America, in their first national convention, invoking upon their action the blessing of Almighty God, put forth in the name and on behalf of the people of this country, the following preamble and declaration of principles:

PREAMBLE

The conditions which surround us best justify our co-operation; we meet in the midst of a nation brought to the verge of moral, political, and material ruin. Corruption dominates the ballot-box, the Legislatures, the Congress, and touches even the ermine of the bench. The people are demoralized; most of the States have been compelled to isolate the voters at the polling places to prevent universal intimidation and bribery. The newspapers are largely subsidized or muzzled, public opinion silenced, business prostrated, homes covered with mortgages, labor impoverished, and the land concentrating in the hands of capitalists. The urban workmen are denied the right to organize for self-protection, imported pauperized labor beats down their wages, a hireling standing army, unrecognized by our laws, is established to shoot them down, and they are rapidly degenerating into European conditions. The fruits of the toil of millions are boldly stolen to build up colossal fortunes for a few, unprecedented in the history of mankind; and the possessors of those, in turn, despise the republic and endanger liberty. From the same prolific womb of governmental injustice we breed the two great classes—tramps and millionaires.

The national power to create money is appropriated to enrich bondholders; a vast public debt payable in legal tender currency has been funded into gold-bearing bonds, thereby adding millions to the burdens of the people.

Silver, which has been accepted as coin since the dawn of history, has been demonetized to add to the purchasing power of gold by decreasing the value of all forms of property as well as human labor, and the supply of currency is purposely abridged to fatten usurers, bankrupt enterprise, and enslave industry. A vast conspiracy against mankind has been organized on two continents, and it is rapidly taking possession of the world. If not met and overthrown at once it forebodes terrible social convulsions, the destruction of civilization, or the establishment of an absolute despotism.

From *The World Almanac*, 1893 (New York: 1893), 83–85. Reprinted in George Brown Tindall, ed., *A Populist Reader, Selections from the Works of American Populist Leaders* (New York: Harper & Row, 1966), 90–96.

We have witnessed for more than a quarter of a century the struggles of the two great political parties for power and plunder, while grievous wrongs have been inflicted upon the suffering people. We charge that the controlling influences dominating both these parties have permitted the existing dreadful conditions to develop without serious effort to prevent or restrain them. Neither do they now promise us any substantial reform. They have agreed together to ignore, in the coming campaign, every issue but one. They propose to drown the outcries of a plundered people with the uproar of a sham battle over the tariff, so that capitalists, corporations, national banks, rings, trusts, watered stock, the demonetization of silver and the oppressions of the usurers may all be lost sight of. They propose to sacrifice our homes, lives, and children on the altar of mammon; to destroy the multitude in order to secure corruption funds from the millionaires.

Assembled on the anniversary of the birthday of the nation, and filled with the spirit of the grand general and chief who established our independence, we seek to restore the government of the Republic to the hands of "the plain people," with which class it originated. We assert our purposes to be identical with the purposes of the National Constitution; to form a more perfect union and establish justice, insure domestic tranquillity, provide for the common defence, promote the general welfare, and secure the blessings of liberty for ourselves and our posterity.

We declare that this Republic can only endure as a free government while built upon the love of the whole people for each other and for the nation; that it cannot be pinned together by bayonets; that the civil war is over, and that every passion and resentment which grew out of it must die with it, and that we must be in fact, as we are in name, one united brotherhood of free men.

Our country finds itself confronted by conditions for which there is no precedent in the history of the world; our annual agricultural productions amount to billions of dollars in value, which must, within a few weeks or months, be exchanged for billions of dollars' worth of commodities consumed in their production; the existing currency supply is wholly inadequate to make this exchange; the results are falling prices, the formation of combines and rings, the impoverishment of the producing class. We pledge ourselves that if given power we will labor to correct these evils by wise and reasonable legislation, in accordance with the terms of our platform.

We believe that the power of government—in other words, of the people—should be expanded (as in the case of the postal service) as rapidly and as far as the good sense of an intelligent people and the teachings of experience shall justify, to the end that oppression, injustice, and poverty shall eventually cease in the land.

While our sympathies as a party of reform are naturally upon the side of every proposition which will tend to make men intelligent, virtuous, and temperate, we nevertheless regard these questions, important as they are, as secondary to the great issues now pressing for solution, and upon which not only our individual prosperity but the very existence of free institutions depend; and we ask all men to first help us to determine whether we are to have a republic to administer before we differ as to the conditions upon which it is to be administered, believing that the forces of reform this day organized will never cease to move forward until every wrong is remedied and equal rights and equal privileges securely established for all the men and women of this country.

PLATFORM

We declare, therefore—

First.—That the union of the labor forces of the United States this day consummated shall be permanent and perpetual; may its spirit enter into all hearts for the salvation of the Republic and the uplifting of mankind.

Second.—Wealth belongs to him who creates it, and every dollar taken from industry without an equivalent is robbery. "If any will not work, neither shall he eat." The interests of rural and civic labor are the same; their enemies are identical.

Third.—We believe that the time has come when the railroad corporations will either own the people or the people must own the railroads, and should the government enter upon the work of owning and managing all railroads, we should favor an amendment to the Constitution by which all persons engaged in the government service shall be placed under a civil-service regulation of the most rigid character, so as to prevent the increase of the power of the national administration by the use of such additional government employees.

FINANCE.—We demand a national currency, safe, sound, and flexible, issued by the general government only, a full legal tender for all debts, public and private, and that without the use of banking corporations, a just, equitable, and efficient means of distribution direct to the people, at a tax not to exceed 2 per cent per annum, to be provided as set forth in the sub-treasury plan of the Farmers' Alliance, or a better system; also by payments in discharge of its obligations for public improvements.

1. We demand free and unlimited coinage of silver and gold at the present legal ratio of 16 to 1.
2. We demand that the amount of circulating medium be speedily increased to not less than $50 per capita.
3. We demand a graduated income tax.
4. We believe that the money of the country should be kept as much as possible in the hands of the people, and hence we demand that all State and national revenues shall be limited to the necessary expenses of the government, economically and honestly administered.
5. We demand that postal savings banks be established by the government for the safe deposit of the earnings of the people and to facilitate exchange.

TRANSPORTATION—Transportation being a means of exchange and a public necessity, the government should own and operate the railroads in the interest of the people. The telegraph, telephone, like the post-office system, being a necessity for the transmission of news, should be owned and operated by the government in the interest of the people.

LAND.—The land, including all the natural sources of wealth, is the heritage of the people, and should not be monopolized for speculative purposes, and alien ownership of land should be prohibited. All land now held by railroads and other corporations in excess of their actual needs, and all lands now owned by aliens should be reclaimed by the government and held for actual settlers only.

EXPRESSION OF SENTIMENTS

Your Committee on Platform and Resolutions beg leave unanimously to report the following:

Whereas, Other questions have been presented for our consideration, we hereby submit the following, not as a part of the Platform of the People's Party, but as resolutions expressive of the sentiment of this Convention.

1. RESOLVED, That we demand a free ballot and a fair count in all elections and pledge ourselves to secure it to every legal voter without Federal Intervention, through the adoption by the States of the unperverted Australian or secret ballot system.

2. RESOLVED, That the revenue derived from a graduated income tax should be applied to the reduction of the burden of taxation now levied upon the domestic industries of this country.

3. RESOLVED, That we pledge our support to fair and liberal pensions to ex-Union soldiers and sailors.

4. RESOLVED, That we condemn the fallacy of protecting American labor under the present system, which opens our ports to the pauper and criminal classes of the world and crowds out our wage-earners; and we denounce the present ineffective laws against contract labor, and demand the further restriction of undesirable emigration.

5. RESOLVED, That we cordially sympathize with the efforts of organized workingmen to shorten the hours of labor, and demand a rigid enforcement of the existing eight-hour law on Government work, and ask that a penalty clause be added to the said law.

6. RESOLVED, That we regard the maintenance of a large standing army of mercenaries, known as the Pinkerton system, as a menace to our liberties, and we demand its abolition. . . .

7. RESOLVED, That we commend to the favorable consideration of the people and the reform press

the legislative system known as the initiative and referendum.

8. RESOLVED, That we favor a constitutional provision limiting the office of President and Vice-President to one term, and providing for the election of Senators of the United States by a direct vote of the people.

9. RESOLVED, That we oppose any subsidy or national aid to any private corporation for any purpose.

10. RESOLVED, That this convention sympathizes with the Knights of Labor and their righteous contest with the tyrannical combine of clothing manufacturers of Rochester, and declare it to be a duty of all who

hate tyranny and oppression to refuse to purchase the goods made by the said manufacturers, or to patronize any merchants who sell such goods.

DRAWING CONCLUSIONS:

1. What does the Omaha Platform suggest about the concerns of farmers in the South and West during the age of industrialization?

2. What can we learn from the Omaha Platform about the reasons many farmers in the South and West abandoned established political parties?

2.2   "SOCKLESS JERRY" SIMPSON, "THE POLITICAL REBELLION IN KANSAS" (1891)

During the 1890s, the state of Kansas was a hotbed of Populism. In 1890, Farmers' Alliance members in Kansas were among the first to break with the old parties and to run independent "Populist" candidates for office. Among the leaders of the farmers' revolt in Kansas was Jeremiah Simpson, nicknamed "Sockless Jerry." In 1890, Simpson was elected to the United States Congress on the Populist ticket. The following year, he published this account of the rise of Populism in Kansas.

GUIDING QUESTIONS:

1.   What sort of portrait does Simpson paint of the emerging industrial order?
2.   What does Simpson say are the grievances of the farmers of Kansas?

THE POLITICAL REBELLION IN KANSAS

By Hon. Jerry Simpson, Member of Congress from the Seventh District of Kansas.

In the campaign of the fall of 1890, in Kansas, a new party sprang into power, which gained strength with a rapidity never before equalled. What was the cause that produced this sudden rebellion against the Republican party? What was the cause of the uprising of the farmers, and what is the remedy for the evils of which they complain? All these are questions pressing for answers; in fact, they must be answered correctly, and the remedy be applied, if this government is to continue to be a free government by the people. It is not always safe, perhaps, to trust a sick man to diagnose his own case; neither can you trust to quacks who profess to cure all ills to which flesh is heir with one quack remedy.

We seem to have once again entered one of those periods in which nations have been confronted with these same questions: like the riddle of the Sphynx, not to answer was to be destroyed. Never before in the history of the world were there such momentous questions; never before in the history of the world was the welfare of the human race so bound up in the solving of these problems. We must now and here settle whether or not we are capable of self-government. We must grapple with, and master, this monster which has eaten up the substance of the producers of wealth in every land. The voters of Kansas are the best representatives of the agricultural class of a half-dozen of the best agricultural States in the Union; they have come West to better their condition; they are a part of that great throng which is always pressing ahead into new countries, trying to escape the oppression of the men who live off their labor; but they find that in Kansas, as in other States, it is impossible to get from under the load which is continually being shifted upon their shoulders, and which grows heavier from year to year. They have found that, in the last twenty-five years, the country, under the control of the great Republican party, has passed into the hands of the money power, the capitalists of the country, who have doubled the oppression of the agricultural classes. Having cried in vain for relief through the Republican and Democratic parties, they are at last driven to desperation, and have resolved to take the political management of the State into their own hands. Out of the necessity

From N. A. Dunning, ed., *The Farmers' Alliance History and Agricultural Digest* (Washington, DC: Alliance Publishing Co., 1891), 280–283.

to adjust these questions grew up the Alliance movement in Kansas.

They began to inquire how it is that in this new State, with its bound-less resources, improved machinery, skilled labor, and its improved means of transportation, the farmers are getting deeper in debt each year; that this new State, that twenty-five years ago was without debt, is now so hopelessly encumbered that it would not sell for enough to pay its debts. This certainly is not caused by the failure of crops, for the crop of Kansas will average with that of any other State in the Union; and Kansas has each year a surplus of wheat, corn, hogs, and cattle.

Some of our public men have said that it was over-production, that we have been raising too much wheat, corn, hogs, and cattle for the world's use. Others have said that it is because the farmers are too extravagant. Others that they are idle and spend their time in talking politics. Others that the farmers do not employ the best methods of farming, and do not understand how to make the soil produce the most with the smallest amount of land and labor. All of which is contradictory and unsatisfactory, and we must look further for the true cause. They made the discovery after they had lighted the lights in school-houses and began to study and discuss these economic questions. They learned that what a farmer wants when he raises a crop of corn and wheat and other products of the farm, is to trade his surplus of such products for the things which he needs; that he must produce on his farm what he must exchange for the products of the manufacturer, and turn them into money value, which represents the value of all articles. He found that, under the present system of trade, he was prevented from making this exchange with the men who would give him the best bargain; that he would be fined, in fact, from forty-seven to fifty-two per cent for his trade, and compelled to trade in the market where there is no competition, where competition has been destroyed by laws passed in the interest of the manufacturer; and through these laws he is forced to bargain with the men who will give him the least of the things he wants for the greatest amount of the things which he does not want, and so he grows poorer and poorer from year to year

and consumes less. As this goes on, the manufacturer making the articles the farmer should consume soon learns that his custom is falling off, and that he must reduce the number of his employees and the wages of those retained. The laborers thus thrown out of employment must also reduce their expenses, and are forced to use less of the products of the farm and factory. In this way is brought about what the political wiseacres call an over-production, which is in fact under-consumption. There is an overproduction of too many farmers, laborers, manufacturers, professional men, merchants, railroads; in fact, too many of everybody. There are particularly too many fools who vote to keep up such a system of government, which obstructs trade and progress, and brings poverty and distress upon the whole land.

Then, again, when the farmer sends his surplus to market the railroads lie in wait for him. In effecting his exchange he must use this great public highway, and he finds that what should be a public blessing is turned into an engine of oppression, and that all the benefits growing out of this great invention are given to the large corporations, which are enabled to rob the people through special privileges granted by laws passed by a Congress whose election has been secured by the free use of money wrung from the people by the charge upon watered stock. Another cause of poverty among the farmers is our system of indirect taxation. Under this system a man is taxed on what he spends, and as the average income of the Western farmer is not more than $500 per annum, he spends at least $350 of this to support his family. One-third of this is taken from him by indirect taxation, or in bounties to capitalists or rich corporations. The balance of his income is used up in paying State and municipal taxes. To cover this loss that falls upon him from year to year, he is forced to take out a mortgage on his farm. Then it is that he falls a prey to the grandest robber of them all, the loan agent or shark, who demands upon a mortgage of $500, in some instances, as high as twenty per cent for securing the loan, and from ten to fifteen per cent for insuring the small buildings on the farm, and then raises doubts about the claimant's right to prove up on it at the land-office, and extracts ten or fifteen per cent for securing the poor settler's title to the land upon which he has lived and worked hard for over five years, in accordance with the homestead law.

The farmer, of course, demurs at this exaction; but the time has come when he must buy improved machinery, and pay debts previously contracted, and the government fees at the land-office before he can prove up. He and his wife, fearing that they must give up the fruits of their labor and struggles to build up a new home, sign the papers, and, after the Shylock's exactions, receive from two to three hundred dollars out of the $500 twelve per cent mortgage, and divide the balance of the swag between the loan agent and the banker, who sells the mortgage, knowing how it has been obtained, to his neighbors, friends, or kinsmen in the East, for the full face of the mortgage, and swaggers around town as a great financier. The mortgage usually contains the provisions that the buildings shall be kept insured, and the taxes paid on the farm, or foreclosure and eviction can be summarily enforced on the settler, leaving him and his family, with his homestead rights to take up public land gone, in a strange land without home or friends.

How could it be possible under such a system that the rich should fail to grow richer and the men of moderate means should rapidly fall into the ranks of the extremely poor? Then is it any wonder that the men who followed "old John Brown" into Kansas, on the principle that it was wrong to rob the black man of the fruits of his toil, should rebel when their own welfare is at stake? It can easily be seen that, after waiting year after year for the Republican party to come to their relief, and each succeeding year seeing relief further off, and that the State had fallen into the hands of the worst political crew that ever cursed any country, under the domineering rule of this arrogant party, controlled by this aristocratic ring of political office-seekers, who cared only for their own advancement, forbearance ceased to be a virtue, and the farmers were wise in resolving to take charge of things themselves. They made the discovery that for long years they had been blinded to their own interests by designing politicians, who kept alive the old war issues and prejudices. They resolved to cast aside the chief apostle of this doctrine of hate, John J. Ingalls, and thereby set an example to the rest of the country, particularly to the South. They saw that new issues would be brought to the front that were pressing for adjustment; therefore it was time to bury the old ones. With this new declaration of independence, called the "St. Louis Demands," they commenced a political revolution that bids fair to sweep from one end of the country to the other, and drive from place and power the men who fattened upon the labor of the people. That this will be no easy task all history will testify; for the oppressor never lets go without a struggle, whether he wields his power through military force, the Church, by controlling money, trade, commerce, transportation, through cunningly devised schemes of legislation, or by holding men in chattel slavery. All history proves that this is the selfish, brutal part of the human race, which knows no law but force.

Now this rebellion in Kansas is against this principle. The people have been driven to it by oppression from the moneyed class of this country. They have served notice upon the politicians of the country that, from this time on, the farmers of this country are going to take a hand in its politics.

DRAWING CONCLUSIONS:

1. What can we learn about the ideas of the Populists from Simpson's article?
2. What can we learn from Simpson's article about the reasons many farmers in the South and West abandoned the established political parties?

2.3 BETTIE GAY, "THE INFLUENCE OF WOMEN IN THE ALLIANCE" (1891)

The National Farmers' Alliance (the organization that gave birth to Populism) was a true social movement that became an important component of the daily lives of its members. In this piece, Bettie Gay (an Alliance member from the state of Texas) discusses the role of women in the Farmers' Alliance. As you read Gay's account of women's role in the Alliance, think about what it reveals about Populism as a social movement and the way it affected the lives of individual farmers. Keep in mind that this was written at a time when women did not have the legal right to vote or hold office.

GUIDING QUESTIONS:

1. What does Gay say are the roles that women play within the Farmers' Alliance?
2. What kind of portrait is she painting of Populism as a social movement?

THE INFLUENCE OF WOMEN IN THE ALLIANCE

BY MRS. BETTIE GAY, COLUMBUS, TEXAS

In the past, woman has been secondary as a factor in society. She has been placed in this position because the people have been educated to believe that she is mentally inferior to the sterner sex. Only of late has the discussion of her social and political rights been brought prominently before the country. The male portion of our population, through a false gallantry, have assumed that they are the protectors of the "weaker sex": women have been led to believe that they had no political or social rights to be respected, and a very large majority of them have bowed in quiet submission.

History proves that the more crude and savage society is, the lower women are placed in the social scale. The men of savage races compel their women to do all the work; in fact, to be their slaves. When this social question is investigated from a scientific standpoint, the wonder is that man has ever been able to emerge from his original condition, while the situation of the mothers of the race has been such as to naturally impede intellectual progress. Only the plain manifestation of the laws of nature and the human mind has enabled man to raise himself above the crude forms of barbarism, and establish what is now termed civilized society.

Education concerning the effects of social conditions is demonstrating that most of the moral evils which afflict society are produced by the unnatural conditions which are imposed upon women. Nature has endowed her with brains; why should she not think? If she thinks, why not allow her to act? If she is allowed to act, what privilege should men enjoy of which she should be deprived? These are pertinent questions which society should begin to consider.

Go into the rural districts, and look at the position occupied by the wives and daughters of the farmers. They have, until of late occupied a social position which tended only to discourage intellectual effort. In most of the churches women have been allowed no voice; and the very moment some brainy woman in a community would rise above her surroundings and take an interest in public questions, the men, as well as the women, would begin to discourage her

From N. A. Dunning, ed., *The Farmers' Alliance History and Agricultural Digest* (Washington, DC: Alliance Publishing Co., 1891), 308–312.

efforts. She would be told by her father, brother, or husband, that such questions are not the concern of women. But the Alliance has come to redeem woman from her enslaved condition, and place her in her proper sphere. She is admitted into the organization as the equal of her brother, and the ostracism which has impeded her intellectual progress in the past is not met with, and men have begun to recognize the fact that, when the women are educated, the battle for human rights will have been fought and won.

Her position in the Alliance is the same as it is in the family,—the companion and helpmeet of man. In it she is given the opportunity to develop her faculties. She is made to feel that she is the equal of man and that she can make herself useful in every department of human affairs; that her mission in the world is more than merely to be called wife or mother (both of which are honorable), but her work is one of sympathy and affection, and her help is as much needed in the great work of reform.

Only in late years have women been considered a necessary factor in reform movements. This has been brought about by advanced thinkers, who have studied sociology and the science of intellectual and moral development. Society seems never to have thought of the fact that there is no progress without opportunity, and that depriving women of their social and political rights has taken from them the inducement to become educated upon great questions. The Alliance contemplates the opening of every avenue of intelligence, which will induce women to become educated, and capable of taking care of themselves in the struggle for existence, and the establishment of a social system which will guarantee to every human being the results of his labor. The condition of the wives and daughters of the farmers is but little better than that of the women who work in factories. In probably a majority of instances, in the South and Southwest, the women assist in cultivating and gathering the crops. Such a condition of industrial serfdom the Alliance, with other reform organizations, expects to overthrow.

In the effort for reform, none can be more interested than women, as they are the chief sufferers whenever poverty or misfortune overtakes the family. They are the ones to look after the welfare of the children of the family. They, more readily than the fathers, see what is necessary to make the family happy and comfortable. But, having been educated to believe that bad conditions are caused by Divine Providence, or are the result of mismanagement, many of them have borne the social evils in silence, and trusted for happiness after they shall have crossed "the silent river."

Through the educational influence of the Alliance, the prejudice against woman's progress is being removed, and within the last five years much has been accomplished in that direction. Women are now recognized as a prominent factor in all social and political movements. In the meetings of the Alliance she comes in contact with educated reformers, whose sympathies she always has. Her presence has a tendency to control the strong tempers of many of the members, and places a premium upon politeness and gentility. She goads the stupid and ignorant to a study of the principles of reform, and adds an element to the organization, without which it would be a failure. Being placed upon an equality with men, and her usefulness being recognized by the organization in all of its work, she is proud of her womanhood, and is better prepared to face the stern realities of life. She is better prepared to raise and educate her offspring, by teaching the responsibility of citizenship and their duty to society.

The meetings give recreation to the mind, and the physical being is for a time relieved from incessant toil. The entire being is invigorated, and the mind is prepared for the reception of much truths as fit her to be companion, mother, and citizen. As stated above, woman has not been considered a factor in great movements, until of late years, but she comes prominently to the front in the Alliance, and demands that she be allowed to render service in the great battle for human rights, better conditions, happier homes, and a higher civilization generally. In fact, she has come to the conclusion that she has some grievances for which remedies should be found, and that she owes it as a duty to herself and society to help work out the social and political salvation of the people.

I believe that there are remedies for most of the evils which afflict society; that poverty and want are the chief causes of crime; and the reason why so many people are found occupying unnatural conditions, is because of the violation of the principles of justice and right, by the government allowing the few to monopolize the land, money, and transportation, which deprives a large portion of the people of their natural right to apply their labor to the gifts of nature. Under such conditions, the people become dependent, hopeless slaves,—a condition which drives the last spark of manhood and womanhood from their bosoms,—and they become outcasts and criminals, and fill our jails and penitentiaries and other places of shame.

It is the duty of the Alliance to consider these questions, and none others are so much interested in the regeneration of society as women. When the battles of life are to be fought, she is always a valiant soldier, and many of them bear upon their faces the scars of the battle with poverty and want. The faces and forms of many of the farmers' wives bear marks of premature age. Their sensibilities are deadened with the cares and toils of life. They have enjoyed but few of the benefits of modern civilization, and but few of the luxuries of life which they have helped to create. They have plodded along, while conscienceless greed has fattened upon their labor, and deprived them of the conditions which are necessary to make them happy and good,—their lives a blessing, their homes a heaven.

But this is a new era in human progress, when woman demands an equal opportunity in every department of life. She is no longer to be considered a tool, a mere plaything, but a human being, with a soul to save and a body to protect. Her mind must be cultivated, that she may be made more useful in the reform movement and the development of the race. It is an acknowledged principle in science that cultivated and intelligent mothers produce brainy children, and the only means by which the minds of the human race can be developed is to strengthen, by cultivation, the intellectual capacities of the mothers, by which means a mentally great race may be produced. When I look into the hard and stolid faces of many of the mothers of the present, and know that they have been deprived of the opportunities which would have improved them, I am not surprised that we are surrounded by people who are the advocates of a system but little better than cannibalism.

Through a system of education, in the Alliance and kindred organizations, we are slowly but surely eradicating the false doctrines of the Dark Ages, and the traditions of the pagans, handed down to us through false teaching. To remove these evils is the grandest work of the age, and the woman who holds herself aloof from reform organizations, either through false pride or a lack of moral courage, is an object of pity, and falls far short of the duty she owes to herself, society, and posterity.

If I understand the object of the Alliance, it is organized not only to better the financial condition of the people, but to elevate them socially, and in every other way, and make them happier and better, and to make this world a fit habitation for man, by giving to the people equal opportunities. Every woman who has at heart the welfare of the race should attach herself to some reform organization, and lend her help toward the removal of the causes which have filled the world with crime and sorrow, and made outcasts of so many of her sex. It is a work in which all may engage, with the assurance that they are entering upon a labor of love, in the interest of the downtrodden and disinherited; a work by which all mankind will be blessed, and which will bless those who are to come after for all time.

The education of the masses is the hope of the world, and a healthy public sentiment must be created in the interest of labor. Poverty must be abolished, and the natural rights of the people must be respected. It is unnecessary for me to pay any tribute to, or heap any abuse upon, woman. She is precisely what her opportunities have made her, whether she is found in a palace or a hovel. She is flesh and blood, and whatever virtues or vices she may possess, can only be attributed to environment and opportunity.

What we need, above all things else, is a better womanhood,—a womanhood with the courage of conviction, armed with intelligence and the greatest virtues of her sex, acknowledging no master and accepting no compromise. When her enemies shall have laid down their arms, and her proper position in society is recognized, she will be prepared to take upon herself the responsibilities of life, and civilization will be advanced to that point where intellect instead of brute force will rule the world. When this work is accomplished, avarice, greed, and passion will cease to control the minds of the people, and we can proclaim, "Peace on earth, good will toward men."

DRAWING CONCLUSIONS:

1. What can we learn from Gay's article about Populism as a social movement?

2.4   POPULIST LETTERS TO THE *COLFAX CHRONICLE* (1890–1891)

Although Grant Parish, Louisiana (Louisiana employs the term "parish" to refer to what other states call "counties") was a hotbed of Populist sentiment in the 1890s, the editor of its local newspaper (the *Colfax Chronicle*) was a staunch Democrat who regularly mocked the People's Party and its local adherents in the pages of the publication. During the early 1890s, the pages of the newspaper were regularly filled with letters to the editor from outraged readers complaining of the plight of the farmers, making the case for Populist ideas, and condemning the editor for his hostility to the movement.

The first document is a letter to the *Chronicle* from a local farmer making the case for the sub-treasury plan proposed by the Farmers' Alliance. The sub-treasury plan would have established federally owned and operated warehouses across the country where farmers could store their crops and receive low-interest government loans. The resistance of the Democratic Party and its elected officials to the sub-treasury plan was a central motivation for southern cotton farmers abandoning the Democrats and embracing the People's Party. In the second document, the editor of the *Chronicle* publishes a resolution from the members of the Farmers' Union in the town of Montgomery endorsing the People's Party. (In Louisiana, the Farmers' Alliance was called the Farmers' Union.) In the third document, a local resident declares the reasons why he believes farmers had to abandon the old political parties and switch their loyalties to the newly organized People's Party.

GUIDING QUESTIONS:

1. What are the grievances of the farmers who are writing to the *Colfax Chronicle*?
2. What reasons do they give for switching their allegiances from the old political parties to the People's Party?
3. There appears to be a great deal of frustration (and even some anger) in these documents. What appears to be the sources of this frustration and anger?

POPULIST LETTERS TO THE *COLFAX CHRONICLE*

A SUB-TREASURY ADVOCATE

Finnville, La., August 19, 1890

Editor Colfax Chronicle:

I am not in the habit of writing newspaper articles, but after reading your editorial on the sub-treasury bill, I will ask admittance to your columns, and I hope you will not consign this to the waste basket, if it is the first attempt of one of your humble "wigwams" friends.

You may say that you "are aware that you will be confronted with that stubborn opposition held in reserve by a large class[?] of your farmer friends, to be poured out on the devoted head of any and all who have the hardihood to think and argue against their pet theories." You are right: we are ready to defend our rights against any and all who oppose the only measure the laboring people have ever asked of the

From the *Colfax Chronicle*, September 6, 1890.

government, unless they will give us a better one. You call it the pet theory. I desire to remind you that the sub-treasury bill is the outgrowth of agrarian thought and sober judgment. "It was the best we could do," said those noble men who framed it. And, Mr. Editor, they never claimed that the laboring people of America were wedded to it. They said, give us this or something better. This is all the farmers of Grant parish want, but this they do want, and want it bad.

. . .

Now, Mr. Editor, about this oath. I like that. It brings us right to the point. Get out of debt, abandon the credit system? How in the name of common sense can we get out of debt, do business on a cash basis, that basis at one hundred dollars to the family of five, and only $5 or $6 per capita in circulation? You ask are we going to foster this sub-treasury borrowing plan. Permit me to answer, yes we will hold to it with a death-like grip until we are given something better. We will work for it, talk for it, write for it, and last but not least, we will vote for it.

In conclusion let me say that this is no child's play. We cannot be put aside by the assertions of unconstitutionality. We are the houses of the farmers passing into the hands of the few. We see everything managed in the interest of the speculator, from the State land office, to the national government. We are monopolies reaping the profits of labor in all of its branches[?]. We have demanded relief, we are told our demands are unconstitutional. Let me say here, there are men who will heed our demands; and, I repeat, we will not let up till they are heeded. We yet have our voices, and we will use them.

A. J. Dunn

EAGER FOR THE FRAY

The following resolutions were unanimously adopted by the Montgomery farmers' union on June 6, 1891. It is a sort of trumpet-blast of would be leaders of the third party in Louisiana. We are of the opinion that wiser counsel will prevail when the State union meets in July, and our Montgomery friends will find they have been entirely too precipitate in resoluting:

Whereas the laboring class of people throughout our entire land and country are sorely oppressed by the present system of laws permitting national banks, railroads and other corporations to control the monied interests of the world; and

Whereas we believe it is wrong to maintain a system of laws by which railroad companies and other corporations are permitted to rob the people of the public domain, which naturally belongs to them and their children for homes for themselves and families and we believe it is wrong to maintain the National Banking system as a medium for the circulation of money as such a system renders it impossible for the people to obtain money except at a high rate of interest, and we believe that the money should come direct to the people and we advocate a system of laws to carry out these views; and

Whereas the people have long since felt these oppressions and discussed their true source, and have persistently plead with the political party in power to right these wrongs and relieve them of the consequent oppression, and

Whereas the people have received only sarcasm, abuse and ridicule from both political parties in answer to their pleadings for relief; and

Whereas we believe these facts to be the real issues of the day and not fanciful or imaginary as claimed by said political parties,

Therefore be it resolved by Montgomery Farmers' Union, No. 90, That we endorse the platform framed by the National Farmers' Alliance at Ocala, Florida and adopted by the National Conference at Cincinnati, Ohio—and

Be it further resolved, that we urge all sub unions and parish unions to adopt a similar resolution.

Be it further resolved, That a copy [of] these resolutions be furnished by the Farmers' Vidette and the Winn Parish Comrade for publication.

B. A. FORTSON, President,
M. L. PAYNE, Secretary.

From the *Colfax Chronicle*, June 27, 1891.

THE INCONSISTENT KICKER

Editor Colfax Chronicle:

I have been laboring under the impression that the farmers of Louisiana had become aroused to the sense of their duty and somewhat educated upon the question of political economy. It was my impression that predomination of English capital, together with other nefarious institutions, should be paramount questions. I was in hopes that the Farmers' State Union would endorse the People's party as being the proper course to pursue in obtaining our freedom from under plutocratic reign. It was surprising indeed, to learn that the State union ignored the Ocala platform, as I thought that every farmers' union had felt the sting of oppression, and was made to realize that our only hope was reform. It is clearly evident that there was a purchase made, and something disposed of at our State union. They simply bartered the hope and success of the People's party for the promise and uncertainty of Tom Adams receiving the governorship of Louisiana.

Brethren, inasmuch as you have decided to stick to the grand old party, there is something necessary for you to do. First, purify the platform and principles of the old party, then you may put pure men in office and expect relief.

There is no question but what both parties of the present age are so corrupt that they have become a stench in God's nostrils. Taking into consideration the sacrifice that was made at Lafayette I have but little hope of the People's party man, now, henceforth and forever. I am a People's party man for this reason: Its platform contains pure and undefiled principles, and will protect the toiling millions from the blighting hand of monopoly, and will enable them to cope successfully with other professions, who are a class of gentlemen sitting upon the throne of their majesty, sucking the very lifeblood of this nation. It is a question without controversy that, if the condition of affairs that now exists continue, in less than fifty years this republic will run into a state of monopoly, subject to the rule of the British sovereign.

Yours truly, S. W. LACROIX.

DRAWING CONCLUSIONS:

1. What can we learn about Populism from these documents?
2. What do these documents suggest about the reasons why many farmers in the South abandoned the old parties in favor of the People's Party?

From the *Colfax Chronicle*, August 22, 1891.

2.5 "WHAT GOD FREELY GIVES TO MAN, MONOPOLY APPROPRIATES" (1895)

This cartoon appeared in a Populist newspaper in Louisiana in 1895. In this context, the word "appropriate" means to take unjustly that which belongs to someone else. A "monopoly" is a large economic entity that controls the market for a good or a service.

GUIDING QUESTIONS:

1. Who or what does the cartoonist blame for the economic difficulties facing many farmers in the 1890s?
2. What sort of portrait is the cartoonist painting of the emerging industrial order?

FIGURE 2. *THE LOUISIANA POPULIST,* "WHAT GOD FREELY GIVES TO MAN, MONOPOLY APPROPRIATES"
From Natchitoches *Louisiana Populist,* May 31, 1895

DRAWING CONCLUSIONS:

1. What can we learn about the ideas of the Populists from this cartoon?
2. What can we learn from this cartoon about the reasons many farmers in the South and West abandoned the established political parties?

2.6 "THE FARMER IS THE MAN" (1927)

"The Farmer is the Man" is a folk song that gained popularity in the late nineteenth century. While the origins of the song are unknown, various versions can be documented being sung in places as far apart as Georgia and Illinois. The first known recording of the song is from the early 1920s. A few years later, a slightly different version appeared in print. It is that version, from the 1927 publication *The American Songbag*, that appears here.

GUIDING QUESTIONS:

1. What portrait does this song paint of the emerging industrial order and the place of farmers within it?
2. What grievances on the part of farmers does this song reflect?

THE FARMER IS THE MAN

(Traditional)

When the farmer comes to town,
With his wagon broken down,
O, the farmer is the man who feeds them all!
If you'll only look and see,
I think you will agree
That the farmer is the man who feeds them all.

The farmer is the man,
The farmer is the man,
Buys on credit till the fall;
Then they take him by the hand,
And they lead him to the land,
And the merchant is the man who gets it all.

The doctor hangs around
While the blacksmith heats his iron,

O, the farmer is the man who feeds them all!
The preacher and the cook
Go strolling by the brook,
And the farmer is the man who feeds them all.

The farmer is the man,
The farmer is the man,
Buys on credit till the fall.
Tho' his family comes to town,
With a wagon broken down,
O, the farmer is the man who feeds them all!

DRAWING CONCLUSIONS:

1. What can we learn from this song about the reasons for the farmers' revolt of the late nineteenth century?

From Carl Sandburg, *The American Songbag* (New York: Harcourt, Brace, and Company, 1927), 282–283.

2.7 WILLIAM ALLEN WHITE, "WHAT'S THE MATTER WITH KANSAS" (1896 AND 1946)

In 1896, William Allen White was a young newspaper editor in Emporia, Kansas. The son of a successful small-town businessman, White was a college graduate at a time when few completed even high school. As Kansas farmers rallied enthusiastically to the Populist cause, White and his newspaper, the Emporia *Gazette*, staunchly defended the economic status quo. In 1896, he achieved national notoriety for an editorial entitled "What's the Matter with Kansas" in which he castigated Populism as a blight on the state. White also denounced Democratic presidential William Jennings Bryan (whom the Populists had endorsed) and his call for a silver-based currency, an inflationary proposal that would help relieve farmers of their debts by raising the prices they received for their products.

In this excerpt from his autobiography, White reproduces the famous editorial and describes the political environment in which it was written. In later years, White came to regret the stance that he took in the 1890s. Nonetheless, the editorial is a testament to the deep political divisions of the United States in that decade. As you read White's piece, you should not expect to understand every specific political reference it makes. Instead focus on what it can tell us about the underlying sources of hostility between the Populists and their opponents.

GUIDING QUESTIONS:

1. How did the young William Allen White view the Populist farmers of 1890s Kansas?
2. Why did he feel such hostility toward Populist farmers?

"WHAT'S THE MATTER WITH KANSAS"

William allen white

W I entered the campaign of 1896, full of wrath and inspired with a fear that became consternation as the campaign deepened. It seemed to me that rude hands were trying to tear down the tabernacle of our national life, to taint our currency with fiat. So, swallowing protection as a necessary evil and McKinley's candidacy as the price of national security, I went into the campaign with more zeal than intelligence, with more ardor than wisdom. The ardor of Kansas was more than a fever. It was a consuming flame. After the nomination of Bryan, which seemed like the swinging of a firebrand in a powder mill, people argued on the streets. The Republicans cried, "Socialists," which would have been a reasonable indictment if they had not immediately followed by calling the Democrats nihilists and anarchists. In offices, on the front porches of the town homes, everywhere the clamor of polities filled the air. I remember one day in July going to Topeka, where in Eugene Ware's office I sat with delight and heard him deliver a diatribe which rang the changes of what ails Kansas or what's wrong with our state.

From *The Autobiography of William Allen White* (New York: MacMillan, 1946), 278–283.

I sat chuckling at his poetic eloquence and told him that I was going to use that in an editorial sometime. He waved his hand and cried:

"Go to it, young man, with my blessing!"

At home I could not walk up Commercial Street without being pulled and hauled by the Populists. I hated wrangling. I never debated anything orally. My answer to argument all my life has been a grin or a giggle or a cocked eye, anything to avoid an acrimonious discussion. Anyway, I have always had to work too hard to bother with the futilities of debate for its own sake.

...

So came Saturday, August 13 [1896].

Early that afternoon I went to the post office for the mail. It was before the days of mail delivery in the town. I remember that I had on my crash suit, which my mother had washed and ironed as she had so many times laundered my father's nankeens. I was dressed to go to Sallie in my best bib and tucker, and I probably looked like a large, white egg as I waddled down the street to the post office, and came back with my arms full of newspaper exchanges. A block from the office a crowd of Populists tackled me. I was impatient and wanted to be on the way. They surrounded me. They were older men—men in their forties and fifties and sixties—and I was twenty-eight. They were shabbily dressed, and it was no pose with them. They were struggling with poverty and I was rather spick-and-span, particularly offensive in the gaudy neckties for which 1 have had an unfortunate weakness. Anyway, they ganged me—hooting, jeering, nagging me about some editorial references I had made. I was froggy in the meadow and couldn't get out, and they were taking a little stick and poking me about. And my wrath must have flamed through my face. Finally I broke through the cordon and stalked, as well as a fat man who toddles can stalk, down the street to the office. I slapped the bundle of mail on Lew Schmucker's desk and sat down to write for Monday's paper an editorial, and I headed it, "What's the Matter with Kanas?" And I remembered what Eugene Ware said and added frill for frill to his ironic diatribe, and it came out pure vitriol:

WHAT'S THE MATTER WITH KANSAS?

Today the Kansas Department of Agriculture sent out a statement which indicates that Kansas has gained less than two thousand people in the past year. There are about two hundred and twenty-five thousand families in his state, and there were ten thousand babies born in Kansas, and yet so many people have left the state that the natural increase is cut down to less than two thousand net.

This has been going on for eight years.

If there had been a high brick wall around the state eight years ago, and not a soul had been admitted or permitted to leave, Kansas would be a half million souls better off than she is today. And yet the nation has increased in population. In five years ten million people have been added to the national population, yet—instead of gaining a share of this say, half a million—Kansas has apparently been a plague spot, and, in the very garden of the world, has lost population by ten thousands every year.

Not only has she lost population, but she has lost money. Every moneyed man in the state who could get out without loss has gone. Every month in every community sees someone who has a little money pack up and leave the state. This has been going on for eight years. Money has been drained out all the time. In towns where ten years ago there were three or four or half dozen money-lending concerns, stimulating industry by furnishing capital, there is now none, or one or two that are looking after the interests and principal already outstanding.

No one brings any money into Kansas any more. What community knows over one or two men who have moved in with more than $5,000 in the past three years? And what community cannot count half a score of men in that time who have left, taking all the money they could scrape together?

Yet the nation has grown rich; other states have increased in population and wealth—other neighboring states. Missouri has gained over two million, while Kansas has been losing half a million. Nebraska has gained in wealth and population while Kansas has gone downhill. Colorado has gained every way, while Kansas has lost every way since 1888.

What's the matter with Kansas?

There is no substantial city in the state. Every big town save one has lost in population. Yet Kansas City, Omaha, Lincoln, St. Louis, Denver, Colorado Springs, Sedalia, the cities of the Dakotas, St. Paul and Minneapolis and Des Moines—all cities and towns in the West—have steadily grown.

Take up the government blue book and you will see that Kansas is virtually off the map. Two or three little scrubby consular places in yellow-fever-stricken communities that do not aggregate ten thousand dollars a year is all the recognition that Kansas has. Nebraska draws about one hundred thousand dollars; little old North Dakota draws about fifty thousand dollars; Oklahoma doubles Kansas; Missouri leaves her a thousand miles behind; Colorado is almost seven times greater than Kansas—the whole west is ahead of Kansas.

Take it by any standard you please, Kansas is not in it.

Go east and you hear them laugh at Kansas; go west and they sneer at her; go south and they cuss her; go north and they have forgotten her. Go into any crowd of intelligent people gathered anywhere on the globe, and you will find the Kansas man on the defensive. The newspaper columns and magazines once devoted to praise of her, to boastful facts and startling figures concerning her resources, are now filled with cartoons, jibes and Pefferian speeches. Kansas just naturally isn't in it. She has traded places with Arkansas and Timbuctoo.

What's the matter with Kansas?

We all know; yet here we are at it again. We have an old mossback Jacksonian who snorts and howls because there is a bathtub in the State House; we are running that old jay for governor. We have another shabby, wild-eyed, rattle-brained fanatic who has said openly in a dozen speeches that "the rights of the user are paramount to the rights of the owner"; we are running him for Chief Justice, so that capital will come tumbling over itself to get into the state. We have raked the old ash heap of failure in the state and found an old human hoop skirt who has failed as a businessman, who has failed as an editor, who has failed as a preacher, and we are going to run him

for Congressman-at-Large. He will help the looks of the Kansas delegation at Washington. Then we have discovered a kid without a law practice and have decided to run him for Attorney General. Then, for fear some hint that the state had become respectable might percolate through the civilized portions of the nation, we have decided to send three or four harpies out lecturing, telling the people that Kansas is raising hell and letting the corn go to weed.

Oh this is a state to be proud of! We are a people who can hold up our heads! What we need is not more money, but less capital, fewer white shirts and brains, fewer men with business judgment, and more of those fellows who boast that they are "just ordinary clodhoppers, but they know more in a minute about finance than John Sherman; we need more men who are posted," who can bellow about the crime of '73, who hate prosperity, and who think, because a man believes in national honor, he is a tool of Wall Street. We have had a few of them some hundred fifty thousand—but we need more.

We need several thousand gibbering idiots to scream about the "Great Red Dragon" of Lombard Street. We don't need population, we don't need wealth, we don't need well-dressed men on the streets, we don't need cities on the fertile prairies; you bet we don't! What we are after is the money power. Because we have become poorer and ornerier and meaner than a spavined, distempered mule, we, the people of Kansas, propose to kick; we don't care to build up, we wish to tear down.

"There are two ideas of government," said our noble Bryan at Chicago. "There are those who believe that if you legislate to make the well-to-do prosperous, this prosperity will leak through on those below. The Democratic idea has been that if you legislate to make the masses prosperous, their prosperity will find its way up and through every class and rest upon them."

That's the stuff! Give the prosperous man the dickens! Legislate the thriftless man into ease, whack the stuffing out of the creditors and tell the debtors who borrowed the money five years ago when money "per capita" was greater than it is now, that the contraction of currency gives him a right to repudiate.

Whoop it up for the ragged trousers; put the lazy, greasy fizzle, who can't pay his debts, on the altar, and bow down and worship him. Let the state ideal be high. What we need is not the respect of our fellow men but the chance to get something for nothing.

Oh, yes, Kansas is a great state. Here are people fleeing from it by the score every day, capital going out of the state by the hundreds of dollars; and every industry but farming paralyzed, and that crippled, because its products have to go across the ocean before they can find a laboring man at work; who can afford to buy them. Let's don't stop this year. Let's drive all the decent self-respecting men out of the state. Let's keep the old clodhoppers who know it all. Let's encourage the man who is "posted." He can talk, and what we need is not mill hands to eat our meat, nor factory hands to eat our wheat, nor cities to oppress the farmer by consuming his butter and eggs and chickens and produce. What Kansas needs is men who can talk, who have large leisure to argue the currency question while their wives wait at home for that nickel's worth of bluing.

What's the matter with Kansas?

Nothing under the shining sun. She is losing her wealth, population and standing. She has got her statesmen, and the money power is afraid of her. Kansas is all right. She has started in to raise hell, as Mrs. Lease advised, and she seems to have an over-production. But that doesn't matter. Kansas never did believe in diversified crops. Kansas is all right. There is absolutely nothing wrong with Kansas. "Every prospect pleases and only man is vile."

I remember even across these years that I slammed the editorial above on the copy spike with a passionate satisfaction that I had answered those farmer hooligans. I was happy and turned to something else for the afternoon.

DRAWING CONCLUSIONS:

1. What can we learn from White's piece about the attitudes many of the economically better off held toward Populism and those who supported it?
2. What can we learn from White's piece about the sources of the deep political divisions between the Populists and their opponents?

CASE STUDIES

One method that historians commonly use to explore a big question is to examine a case or a series of cases. A case is a detailed example that one studies in depth to shed light on the strengths and weaknesses of various positions on the big question. As you read each case study, ask yourself what it reveals about the sources of the political and social turmoil that accompanied industrialization in the late 1800s.

3.1 THE HOMESTEAD STRIKE OF 1892

The first case study is the Homestead Strike of 1892, among the most significant labor disputes of the late nineteenth century. It pitted the Carnegie Steel Company, the country's leading steel producer, against members of the Amalgamated Association of Iron and Steel Workers (the AA), a union that represented skilled workers in the iron and steel industries. For many years, the company and the AA had successfully negotiated contracts that determined such matters as wages, working conditions, and job duties. In 1892, however, contract talks between the union and the company broke down. Shortly thereafter, Henry Clay Frick (the company's general manager and Andrew Carnegie's right-hand man) announced that Carnegie Steel would no longer engage in negotiations with the AA. While the immediate point of conflict revolved around wage levels, the company was also concerned that the work rules negotiated by the union impeded management's ability to implement more efficient production methods.

Our account of the strike comes from Arthur G. Burgoyne, a Pittsburgh-based journalist who published a book-length study of the dispute in 1893. The account begins with the breakdown in contract negotiations and ends with the July 6th battle on the grounds of the steel plant. As you read this account of the Homestead Strike, ask yourself why this labor dispute escalated to the point of violence.

GUIDING QUESTIONS:

1. What specific issues were in dispute between Carnegie Steel and the Amalgamated Association?
2. Why weren't these issues resolved through compromise and negotiation?
3. What led to the violence between Pinkerton security forces and residents of the town of Homestead on July 6, 1892?

EXCERPTS FROM *HOMESTEAD: A COMPLETE HISTORY OF THE STRUGGLE OF JULY, 1892*

ARTHUR G. BURGOYNE

CHAPTER 3

. . .

LOCKED OUT

On June 15, the convention of the Amalgamated Association completed the general wage scale for iron mills and presented it to the manufacturers' committee. The manufacturers responded by producing a scale of their own, embodying extensive reductions. This was the beginning of a dispute, stubborn on both sides, which was kept up long after the final adjournment of the convention, that body assigning the duty of conferring with the manufacturers to a special wage committee.

The consideration of the scales for steel mills, including that prepared by the Homestead lodges, was not completed by the convention until June 23. On that day, a committee, headed by William Roberts,

---

From Arthur G. Burgoyne, *Homestead: A Complete History of the Struggle of July, 1892 between the Carnegie Steel Company, Limited, and the Amalgamated Association of Iron and Steel Workers* (Pittsburgh, PA: Rawsthorne Engraving and Printing Co., 1893), 31–70.

one of the most intelligent of the Homestead mill workers, appeared at the offices of the Carnegie Company, on Fifth Avenue, Pittsburgh, and was escorted to Mr. H. C. Frick's private room. Mr. Frick, General Manager Potter, H. L. Childs and F. T. F. Lovejoy acted for the company in the conference which followed. Mr. Roberts, acting as spokesman for his colleagues, presented the Homestead scale as approved by the convention, and explained that the employees were prepared to concede several points, admitting, however, of no reduction exceeding 15 per cent, in any department. The men were willing even to reduce the minimum selling price of billets on which the rate of wages should be estimated to $24 per ton, but the firm insisted upon the $23 rate, which, as previously explained, signified a serious depression in wages.

The conference, after a discussion lasting several hours, broke up without accomplishing anything.

The following day, June 24, had been fixed by Mr. Frick as the last on which the Carnegie firm would treat with its employees as members of the Amalgamated Association. The day passed without a conference. It was believed, however, that, in view of the concessions which the men had stated their willingness to make, even though they refused to make the complete surrender which Mr. Frick demanded, the firm would consent to fresh conferences with the committee. Yet the fact that the firm, which had sufficient orders on hand to keep the mill busy for many months, was canceling these orders, coupled with the extraordinary preparations for warfare which were being made at the mills, cast a damper on the hopes of the men. There was hardly a ray of sunshine to brighten the gloomy outlook.

On June 25, Mr. Lovejoy, secretary of the Carnegie Company, stated through the newspapers that the conferences were at an end, that the firm had decided to make the rate of $23 a ton on billets the basis of wages, and that this rate would be enforced without regard to the opinion of the Amalgamated Association. It was also the intention to change the time of fixing the wage schedule from June to January, so that if a strike or lock-out should occur, the hardships of the winter season would strengthen the company's hand. So, at least, the men interpreted the proposed change.

Mr. Lovejoy's statement, although given out in an informal way, was generally accepted as meaning that the ax was forthwith to be let fall upon the neck of organized labor at Homestead, and that no human power could stay the hand of the executioner.

Still all was quiet at Homestead. June 25 was Saturday and pay-day, but the day was marked by less activity and bustle than usual. The stores were not crowded, and little money was spent. In the face of trouble, the end of which it was impossible to foresee, men carefully put away the contents of their pay envelopes. The wolf might come to the door before long and resources had to be husbanded. Few cared for the little Saturday jollifications common at other times. Wherever a group of mill men came together, the one theme of discussion was the ultimatum of the firm, the prospect of a wholesale discharge of union men on July 1 and the meaning of the warlike equipment of the mill property.

A new and significant name was devised for the Carnegie enclosure, with its ramparts, watch towers, search-lights and other suggestions of war, and flew from mouth to mouth with the rapidity of lightning.

"Fort Frick."

An ill-omened name it was, bristling with offensive associations; but its propriety as a descriptive epithet could not be questioned.

Who was to occupy the "fort?" Whose guns were to be used through those loopholes?

"Pinkerton detectives," said some, and the rumor that an army of "Pinkertons" had been hired and might already be on its way to garrison the works and shed the blood of the men of Homestead found ready credence and deepened the feeling of resentment abroad in the town. Many were disposed to believe that Pinkerton scouts had arrived and were making things ready for the coming of the main guard.

On Tuesday, June 28, the company ordered the armor-plate mill and the open-hearth department shut down, throwing 800 men out of employment.

This was the beginning of the lock-out, for a lock-out it was, and not a strike, as has been very generally represented.

A strike occurs when dissatisfied workingmen cease work of their own accord and refuse to return until the cause of dissatisfaction is removed.

A lock-out originates with the employing individual or corporation, and consists in the refusal to let the employees work until they come to terms with the employer.

As Mr. Frick took the initiative, the trouble at Homestead was distinctively a lock-out, although, if Mr. Frick had chosen, he could have permitted it to take the form of a strike.

It made little difference in the end which of the contestants took the first aggressive step. Once the Frick ultimatum was promulgated, a struggle was inevitable, and if the firm had not thrown down the gauntlet, the men most assuredly would have forced the fighting on their own account.

The night of June 28 witnessed strange scenes in Homestead. The pent-up feelings of the men now found vent unrestrainedly. Effigies of Frick and Potter were hung on telegraph poles. Denunciations of the firm and its policy were heard on every hand. Knots of angry men gathered outside the board fence that hedged the mill enclosure, peered through the loop-holes at the watchmen on duty within and talked defiantly of what would happen if the methods that triumphed over the poor, disorganized serfs in the coke regions were to be tried upon four thousand sturdy and intelligent steelworkers. If an apostle of non-unionism had ventured upon the streets of Homestead that night he would have fared badly.

The next morning, at the call of the officers of the local lodges, 3,000 steelworkers met in the opera house. The chairman of the executive committee stated to the meeting that, at a conference of committeemen representing the eight lodges, held on the preceding evening, it had been decided to submit the question of shutting down the mechanical department of the mills to the steelworkers *en masse*, irrespective of affiliation with the lodges, and that the decision thus arrived at should be binding on all. This report was approved and a motion was made that a committee be appointed to request the mechanics and day laborers to quit work at once. A workman asked if the watchmen were to be included, and another answered: "Three years ago the watchmen wanted to come out and now they *must* come."

The motion passed amid tremendous cheering.

. . .

A motion to appoint a press committee, consisting of one member from each of the eight lodges, was carried after a discussion as to unreliable reports. The membership of this committee was kept secret for the time being.

A whirlwind of excitement was roused when a speaker told of a report that 200 non-union workmen were coming to Homestead disguised in the blue uniform of Pinkerton detectives. "Watch the depots," was the unanimous cry that followed this alarmist statement.

When, after a session of two hours, the meeting adjourned, there remained not the least doubt as to the unity of feeling among all classes of workers in the town. Every man was ready to enter upon relentless strife, and if there was a coward or malingerer in any quarter, he wisely held his peace.

After the general meeting, the eight lodges held a secret session, at which an advisory committee was appointed, with full power to direct the workmen's campaign.

. . .

Special committees were appointed to patrol the river stations and all entrances to the town. The patrols were directed to cover their beats night and day and report to the advisory committee. Arrangements were also made to have the river patrolled in skiffs, and the steamboat "Edna" was secured to aid in this service.

Headquarters were established in a commodious public hall, with accommodations for telegraph operators, the committee being expected to maintain communication with all parts of the country, so as to obtain instant information of any movement of non-union men designed for service at Homestead. The liquor saloons were visited and the proprietors requested to use special precautions against the promotion of drunkenness and disorderly gatherings, under pain of being required to close their establishments.

Eight effigies of Carnegie officials were cut down by the committee, and notice was given that persons outraging decency in this manner in the future would be disciplined.

The burgess of the town, John McLuckie, was informed that he might call upon the Amalgamated Association for whatever number of men he might deem necessary to assist him in preserving the peace.

In short, the government of Homestead had now passed absolutely into the hands of the advisory committee of the Amalgamated lodges, and the committee was determined to use its arbitrary authority for the preservation of order and decency and the protection of life and property as well as the exclusion from Homestead of non-union men, better known to the unionist as "scabs" or "black sheep."

On July 2 the entire force of employees at the Carnegie mills was paid off and served with notices of discharge.

With the exception of a slight altercation between General Manager Potter and some of the men who were guarding one of the gates of the mill there was no disorder.

Secretary Lovejoy now made his final statement on behalf of the firm declaring the mill to be permanently non-unionized. "Hereafter," he said, "the Homestead steel works will be operated as a non-union mill. We shall not recognize the Amalgamated Association of Iron and Steel Workers in our dealings with the men. The mill will be an open one where all men may work regardless of their affiliation with a labor organization. There will be, no doubt, a scale of wages; but we shall deal with the men individually; not with any organization. Such a thing as a union will not be recognized. There will be no further conferences with the Amalgamated Association."

The mammoth steel plant was now deserted, except by a few watchmen and the government steel inspectors, with whom the advisory committee did not interfere.

The locked-out men were perfectly organized and ready to fight against any odds at a moment's notice. A report that strangers were on the way to Homestead along either of the railroads brought a battalion of stalwart fellows to the stations on the outskirts.

Mr. Frick might as well have undertaken to storm Gibraltar as to introduce a force of non-unionists into the town.

. . .

CHAPTER 4
THE PINKERTONS

WHILE Mr. Frick's men were busily engaged in perfecting a martial organization and putting the government of the town of Homestead on a war footing,

Mr. Frick himself was not idle. He did not waste any time in considering projects for immediately introducing non-union men into the mills, being well aware that, if men foolhardy enough to take the risk of "blacksheeping" at Homestead could be found, it would still be impracticable to get them past the picket lines of the locked-out steelworkers, and that, even if a force of non-unionists could be piloted into the mill their presence would be the signal for an attack by the union men and possibly for the destruction of the firm's property.

Mr. Frick had another plan—a plan suggested by his successful encounters with the Connellsville coke-workers. He conceived the idea of garrisoning "Fort Frick" with a sufficient number of armed and disciplined Pinkerton guards to hold any attacking force at bay and later on to bring in non-union workmen under cover of the Pinkerton men's rifles.

How long this project had been maturing in the mind of the Carnegie Company's chairman cannot be told. Certain it is that he had made up his mind to carry it out long before he met the wage conference committee for the last time, and that when, on June 23, he went through the form of a discussion with Mr. Roberts and Mr. Roberts' confreres, he had not the least notion of coming to any kind of an understanding other than that which might be brought about by force.

Mr. Frick was too well acquainted with the estimation in which the Pinkerton men are held by the labor unions to underrate the import of his action, and can hardly have been ignorant of the fact that in bringing on these myrmidons, he was making doubly sure of sanguinary times at Homestead.

A sketch of the personnel and methods of the "Pinkerton National Detective Agency," as it is styled by its chiefs, will make clear to the reader the reasons for the hatred and contempt entertained for this body by workingmen everywhere.

The agency was founded in 1850 by Allan Pinkerton, a young Scotchman, who had been brought into public notice at Elgin, Ill., by his success in ferreting out a counterfeiter. Allan Pinkerton's fame as a detective became national. He organized a war secret service, was trusted by Lincoln, whose life he once saved; by Grant and other national leaders in war times, and aroused continual interest by his strokes of skill and daring. The enterprise from which sprang the Pinkerton "standing army" of to-day was set on foot in a shabby little office in La Salle Street, Chicago, and there the headquarters of the agency still remain.

Pinkerton detectives came into great request and were soon engaged in the unraveling of crimes and the hunting down of criminals all over the continent. Allan Pinkerton meanwhile discerned a fresh source of profit and turned it to account by hiring out his men as watchmen for banks and great commercial houses. The "Pinkerton Preventive Watch," composed of trained men, uniformed and armed, and acting independently of the municipal police, was established.

The emblem adopted by the agency was a suggestive one. It consisted of an eye and the motto, "We never sleep."

As old age came on Allan Pinkerton and his business kept growing, he turned over the work of supervision to his sons, William A. and Robert A. Robert was placed in charge of a branch bureau in New York and William remained in Chicago. Agencies with regular forces of men were established in Philadelphia, Boston, St. Paul, Kansas City and Denver. By communication with these centres, the chiefs could control, at a few days' notice, a force of 2,000 drilled men, and this could be expanded by drawing on the reserves registered on the books of the agency for service on demand, to 30,000, if necessary,—more men than are enrolled in the standing army of the United States.

When a large number of recruits is needed, the Pinkertons usually advertise in the newspapers asking for able-bodied men of courage, but without stating for whose service. In New York, prospective recruits are brought to a building on lower Broadway where the Pinkertons have an armory, stocked with Winchester rifles, revolvers, policemen's clubs and uniforms. After the number of men needed is secured, the addresses of the eligible applicants for whom there are no places are taken and they are notified to hold themselves in readiness for a future call. Men who have served in the army or as policemen receive the preference.

Pinkerton detectives have no real authority to make arrests. They are rarely sworn in as special constables or as deputy sheriffs and the uniform which they wear is merely for show.

Of late years they have been employed very frequently to protect the property of great manufacturing corporations during strikes or lock-outs. This is, without exception, the most trying and perilous service which they have to undergo. The pay is good, however, the rate agreed upon for duty at Homestead, for example, being $5 a day for each man.
. . .

In recent years, the conversion of the guards into an irresponsible military organization, with self-constituted authority to overawe striking workmen has provoked a feeling of intense hatred on the part of organized labor towards these soldier-policemen. Attempts to abolish the Pinkerton system by legislation have succeeded in only a few states, New York and New Jersey among the number, for the reason that the corporations which find use for armed mercenaries have sufficient wealth and influence to control legislative action.
. . .

As has already been told, the men of Homestead entertained a profound abhorrence of the Pinkertons and were resolved to push resistance to any extreme rather than permit themselves to be whipped into submission by armed hirelings. They had no knowledge of Mr. Frick's dealings with the agency, although their familiarity with the Frick policy in the coke regions, coupled with the equipment of the mill property for occupation by a garrison excited a well-defined suspicion of what was coming.

Mr. Frick gave the final order for a supply of guards in a letter written to Robert A. Pinkerton, of New York, on June 25, the day after his meeting with the wage committee from the Amalgamated convention. The order was given in as matter-of-fact a manner as if the Carnegie chairman were bespeaking a supply of coke or pig-iron.

"We will want 300 guards," he wrote, "for service at our Homestead mills as a measure of precaution against interference with our plan to start the operation of the works again on July 6, 1892."

"These guards," Mr. Frick went on to direct, "should be assembled at Ashtabula, O., not later than the morning of July 5, when they may be taken by train to McKees Rocks, or some other point on the Ohio River below Pittsburgh, where they can be transferred to boats and landed within the enclosures of our premises at Homestead. We think absolute secrecy essential in the movement of these men, so that no demonstration can be made while they are en route."

As Mr. Frick acknowledged in his letter the receipt of "your favor of the 22d," it was evident that the negotiations with the Pinkerton agency had been pending for some time.

Immediately after having despatched his order for a Pinkerton battalion, Mr. Frick sent for Captain Rodgers, of the towboat Little Bill, and directed him to fit up two barges with sleeping accommodations and provisions for 300 men, who were to be taken on board at some point not then determined, brought to the works at Homestead, and subsequently lodged and boarded on the barges.

He also notified the sheriff of Allegheny county, William H. McCleary, through Messrs. Knox & Reed, attorneys for the Carnegie Company, that there would be a strike at Homestead and that 300 Pinkerton watchmen had been engaged, and requested the sheriff to deputize the entire force; that is to say, to appoint them police agents of the county. The sheriff maintained afterwards that, on the advice of his attorney, he had declined to deputize the Pinkerton men until they should be installed in the mill and had reserved the right to act at his discretion when that time came. Mr. Frick, on the other hand, declared on the witness stand that the sheriff consented to deputize the men and assigned his chief deputy to swear them in.

The train was now laid; the fuse was lit, and all that remained to be done in the Carnegie camp was to wait for the explosion.

To disarm suspicion on the other side, however, Mr. Frick, as the crisis approached, gave out information leading the public in general and the locked-out men in particular to believe that he meant to rely on the ordinary processes of law to protect him in the non-unionizing of his works. On the evening of July 4, after a conference with the other chief officers of the firm, he furnished a statement to the newspapers alleging that there was no trouble to be feared, that the men were weakening, a large number of them being anxious to get back to work, and that the plant would be placed in the hands of the county, the sheriff being requested to furnish enough deputies to ensure adequate protection.

With all his firmness, the doughty chairman of the Carnegie Company dared not make a clean breast of his program. The way for the *coup de grace* had to be cleared by strategy and dissimulation.

The locked-out men celebrated Independence Day with due patriotic fervor. The force of guards was increased from 350 to 1,000, the picket system being expanded so as to form an outline five miles in extent, covering both sides of the river.

. . .

And now from a score of cities came the Pinkerton myrmidons to the headquarters at Chicago, few among them knowing or caring on what mission they were bound, as long as they got their daily rations and their daily pay, but all comprehending that blind obedience was the watchword. Captain F. H. Heinde had been detailed to take charge of the expedition, and under his guidance the men proceeded from Chicago to Youngstown, and thence to Bellevue, on the Fort Wayne railroad, opposite the Davis Island dam, arriving at this point at 10:30 o'clock on the evening of July 5.

Early in the day, Mr. Frick had issued final orders to Captain Rodgers, directing him to tow his two barges down the Ohio River to the dam in time to meet the battalion of Pinkerton guards. Captain Rodgers duly carried out his orders. With the boats Little Bill and Tide, each having a barge in tow, he arrived at the dam at 10 P. M. There he was met by Colonel Joseph H. Gray, Sheriff McCleary's chief deputy, who had been dispatched by the sheriff to "keep the peace," if his own testimony and that of the sheriff are to be accepted, whereas, according to Mr. Frick's story, his real mission was to deputize the Pinkerton guards and thus render the county liable for the acts of these strangers.

At 10:30 P. M., the trainload of guards arrived; the men embarked in the barges; the Little Bill and the Tide puffed away as cheerfully as if they were towing a pleasure party, and in the stillness of the beautiful

July night the expedition moved slowly in the direction of Homestead.

CHAPTER 5

THE FIRST SHOT

THE barges on which Captain Heinde and his 300 men embarked were primitive specimens of the boat builders' art, previously used for the transportation of freight. Unlike the ordinary coal barge, these were roofed in, and, were it not for the flat roof, would have exactly resembled Noah's ark. They measured 125 feet long and 20 feet wide. One was known as the Iron Mountain; the other as the Monongahela. These floating barracks had been purchased a week before the time of the Pinkerton expedition by an agent of Mr. Frick's, and quietly fitted up at the landing-place. . . .

. . .

At the last moment a number of mysterious looking cases were put on board. These contained Winchester rifles and had been forwarded to the Carnegie Company by Adams Express. Watchmen at the landing met all inquiries with the explanation that the barges were intended for the transportation of laborers to the Beaver dam on the Ohio River.

It has been said that most of the Pinkerton men had no idea of the nature of their mission. The fact is that only the officers of the expedition comprehended the gravity of the work in hand. However, when the men found themselves being conveyed up the river in the close quarters which the barges afforded to so large a number, many of them became uneasy, and, weary as they were after their long trip by rail, but few were able to close an eye.

As the barges approached the mouth of the Monongahela River, the lights of the two great cities of Pittsburgh and Allegheny illuminated the surface of the waters; but no midnight wayfarer who saw the Little Bill and the Tide, with their odd-looking tows, dreamt for an instant that within those coffin-like craft was the Frick army of invasion and that, within a few hours, those same craft would harbor terror, bloodshed and death. The two cities slept on, unconscious of the thunderbolt that was to fall at the dawning of the day.

When the boats drew near the Smithfield Street bridge, which connects South Pittsburgh with the city proper, there were, however, keen eyes to note their coming. A scout from Homestead, who was one of a detail appointed to look out for suspicious movements along the Pittsburgh wharves under the cover of night, detected the ominous procession and, hurrying to a telegraph office, wired the warning to Homestead: "Watch the river. Steamer with barges left here." On receipt of this news, the advisory committee prepared to issue a general alarm at five minutes' notice. The belief at headquarters was that 100 special deputies were on the way to take charge of the mill under orders from the sheriff.

. . .

At 3 A. M. the barges reached the B. & O. railroad bridge at Glenwood. Day was breaking, but a heavy fog overhung the water, so that the barges were not visible from the shore; nor could the watchers on deck perceive what was going on a few hundred yards away on the Homestead side of the river.

Yet, while the signs of danger were hidden from the eye, there were manifestations, the significance of which could not be misunderstood.

The voices of men, women and children were heard breaking in harshly upon the stillness of the early morning. Scout called to scout almost loudly enough for their words to be caught by the listeners on the water.

Captain Heinde, although a brave man, and used to dangerous situations, felt a sinking of the heart at this unmistakable proof that the secret of the expedition was no longer a secret and that if a landing was to be made at Homestead, it would have to be gained by fighting for it.

A feeling of alarm seized upon the green hands among the guards. There was danger in the air, and numerous as they were, what chance was there for self-defense as long as they were cooped up within four walls? It took the utmost tact and firmness on the part of the experienced guards, who served as officers, to calm the anxious ones and lead them to believe that they would soon reach safe quarters on *terra firma*.

About this time, a horseman riding at breakneck speed, dashed into the streets of Homestead giving the alarm as he sped along. In a few minutes the news that barges, supposed to be filled with deputies, were nearing the town had spread far and near and, with one accord, the people rushed to the river bank. Here, for two hours that seemed like weeks, thousands of men and women waited for the arrival of the enemy—a dangerous enemy, they felt sure, judging by the manner of his coming.

As the barges drew nearer to Homestead, the noise on the shore grew louder and louder and soon the sharp crack of rifles rang out, giving a foretaste of what was in store for the unwelcome visitors. Whether these shots, which were fired before the Pinkertons attempted to land, were intended as signals or were aimed, in a random way, at the barges has never been determined. There is no doubt, however, that the firing from the bank stopped as soon as the Little Bill and its tow drew up opposite the mill landing.

This landing was on the beach within the mill enclosure, Mr. Frick having had the wire-topped fence carried down to low-water mark, so as to shut off all access by land. Above the landing-place frowned a steep eminence largely composed of slag and other refuse from the mill. At this point, also, rise the piers of an iron bridge, over which the P., McK. & Y. railroad runs into the mill yard. This bridge is familiarly known at Homestead as the "Pemickey."

No sooner did the waiting multitude on the river bank perceive that the occupants of the barges meant to put in at the Carnegie Company's landing-place than, with a roar of anger, strong men tore down the fence that barred their path, and ran to the spot where, had they delayed five minutes longer, the Pinkerton men would have disembarked in safety.

Prior to this time the workmen had religiously refrained from trespassing upon the company's property. It had been their set purpose to avoid the odium which would attach to any act suggesting vandalism or arbitrary assaults upon property rights.

But now was not the time to think of conservative methods. Who could tell what kind of invaders were in those ugly-looking barges?

Were they deputies whom the sheriff sought to bring in like a thief in the night? Were they—and at this thought every man's blood boiled—a regiment of Pinkertons brought there to repeat the Pinkerton exploits of a few years before in the coke regions?

What were the odds, one way or the other? Whoever the visitors were, they came with every manifestation of an evil purpose, and was not self-preservation the first law of nature, applying as such to a Homestead steelworker in danger of losing his job and, perhaps, his home?

So the fence went down, and the straight road from the river to the mill was blockaded by a band of resolute fellows that neither Pinkerton men nor sheriff's deputies could hope to overcome.

The scene at this time within the barge Iron Mountain, which had been towed close to the shore, was one of wild confusion. The plan of a secret landing had been frustrated, and there was nothing for it now but a hand-to-hand conflict against terrible odds.

The cases of rifles were broken open and these weapons and revolvers were hastily distributed among the men. About fifty men were armed with clubs. Captain John W. Cooper, of the New York and Philadelphia division, Captain Charles Norton, of the Chicago division, and Captain Heinde, who had general charge of the expedition, supervised these arrangements. When all were in readiness for battle, a gangplank was shoved out and the three captains stepped forward, with Heinde in the van. Twenty of the rank and file appeared behind them on the bow of the boat.

At this offensive move, the Homestead men, most of whom were armed, shouted a fierce warning.

"Go back," they cried, "go back, or we'll not answer for your lives."

There were blue uniforms among the group on the bow of the Iron Mountain, and these told their own story to the excited people on the shore.

For a moment the Pinkerton men stood at bay. The scene before them was one to appall the bravest. On the beach several hundred men and women—for mothers, wives and sisters had joined in the mad rush to the landing-place—some of them half dressed, some carrying loaded guns, some with stones or clubs in their hands; in the distance hundreds more rushing to the defense; in the background a huge embankment intercepting the passage to the mills; behind them the river and the chance of saving themselves by flight. Retreat, however, would have been ruinous to the prestige of the Pinkerton agency besides resulting probably in throwing upon the agency the entire cost of the fruitless expedition, for Mr. Frick would hardly be willing to pay for services not even fairly begun.

So the warning of the workmen was disregarded, and, with a word of command to his men, Captain Heinde pressed forward.

Suddenly a shot was fired—whether from the barges or from the shore has always been a mystery.

Captain Cooper turned instantly towards the barges and in a loud voice gave the order: "Fire!"

A score of Winchester rifles were discharged into the crowd on the bank with deadly effect. Several of the workmen were seen to fall. The first blood had been shed and now the one thought of the men of Homestead was *vengeance,* merciless and complete, on the strangers who had come to shoot them down.

The volley fired from the barges was repaid with interest, and when the smoke from the answering discharge cleared away it was seen that havoc had been wrought on the barges. Captain Heinde had been shot through the leg; J. W. Kline and another detective were mortally wounded and perhaps a dozen others on the Pinkerton side were wounded more or less severely. The Little Bill was fairly riddled with bullets, and Captain Rodgers, having taken the injured men off the barges, lost no time in steaming away from his uncomfortable quarters, leaving the Pinkertons to land, if they could, and if not, to remain where they were and make the best of a desperate situation.

Both sides now withdrew, the workmen abandoning their exposed position, where they offered an easy target to the marksmen on the barges, and establishing themselves on the heights, while the Pinkertons retired into the barges and proceeded to prepare for renewed action by cutting loopholes in the sides of the craft. It would have been suicidal to attempt another sally.

. . .

The workmen now occupied themselves with the construction of ramparts out of pig and scrap iron. Enough of these were piled up to accommodate scores of sharpshooters. Men armed with rifles also took positions at various points of vantage in

the mill buildings and a desultory fire was kept up. At the same time armed men appeared on the other side of the river and began a fusillade on the barges. The non-combatants—men, women and children to the number of about 5,000—thronged the steep hills which rise above Homestead, whence they had an unobstructed view of what was taking place in the mill yard and on the river.

. . .

At the Carnegie offices there were no signs of perturbation, although Mr. Frick and his associates were early informed of the bloody outcome of their scheme of invasion. President Weihe, of the Amalgamated Association, urged a conference with the men as the only expedient which might be successfully employed to stop the shedding of blood.

The answer to this humane suggestion was characteristic. It was a flat refusal.

. . .

Four thousand infuriated steelworkers and three hundred caged Pinkertons were to be left to fight out their deadly quarrel without let or hindrance.

The dictates of law and humanity were alike suspended upon that July day—the most unfortunate day in the history of organized labor in the United States.

CHAPTER 6
THE BOMBARDMENT

While the heroes of the battle at the landing were building breastworks in the mill-yards and keeping up an intermittent fire on the enemy, a busy scene was in progress at the telegraph office in the advisory committee's headquarters. Here a temporary arsenal was established and rifles, shot guns and ammunition were distributed to volunteers eager to take a hand against Mr. Frick's emissaries.

Soon a new terror was added to those already menacing the Pinkertons. The dull roar of a cannon was heard proceeding from the heights across the river, and, at the first shot, a huge gap was torn in the roof of the outer barge. Another shot flew wide of the barges and struck Silas Wain, a young steelworker who was standing in an exposed part of the mill yard, killing him instantly. Wain's sweetheart, a young English girl named Mary Jones, to whom he was to have been married in a few weeks, almost lost her reason when the news of her lover's death reached her, and was delirious for hours. In consequence of this unfortunate occurrence, the cannon that did the mischief—a twenty-pounder—was subsequently shipped across to the Homestead side. Another piece of ordnance, of smaller caliber, was taken from the quarters of the Homestead Grand Army post and mounted at the pump-house of the county poor farm, adjoining the mill-yard. Owing to the elevation of the position, however, and the inexperience of the men who were handling the guns, it was found impossible to get the range of the barges and both pieces were ultimately abandoned.

As the morning advanced, the workmen began to realize that some more effective means than rifle bullets must be resorted to in order to dispose of the barges and their obnoxious freight. The Pinkertons took care not to expose themselves, unless when one more venturesome than the rest undertook to make a reconnaissance and emerged on the bow of either barge. As this exploit invariably attracted a hail of bullets it was not frequently attempted. About 50 of the guards, all of them old hands in the Pinkerton service, kept up a regular fire through the loopholes cut in the sides of the barges, rendering it unsafe for a workman to show himself outside the furnace-stacks and piles of metal used as ramparts. George Rutter, an old and respected Amalgamated man and a member of the Grand Army, forfeited his life by taking chances on the accuracy of the Pinkerton men's marksmanship. He was shot in the thigh and died from the wound a few days later. John Morris, another millworker, and Henry Striegel, a young man who was on the field merely as a sympathizer, met the same fate. Striegel accidentally shot himself with his own gun, and was struck by shots from the barges after he fell.

Shortly after 11 o'clock, the Little Bill steamed back towards the landing-place flying the Stars and Stripes, Captain Rodgers having conceived the idea that the mill men would not dare to fire on the national flag, despite its being hoisted above a hostile craft. The captain's mind was speedily disabused of this idea. Volley after volley was poured into the little steamer, smashing the glass in the pilot-house and making the splinters fly in all directions. The man at the wheel, Alexander McMichaels, had to abandon his post and rush below. John T. McCurry, who had been hired the day before as watchman on the boat, without being informed of the kind of service in prospect, was shot in the groin, and Captain Rodgers only saved his life by throwing himself on his face on the deck. According to the story told afterwards, the Captain had purposed connecting with the barges and releasing them from their perilous position, but was glad enough to run the gauntlet with his own boat without attempting to relieve others.

The Little Bill arrived at a moment when the escape of the Pinkertons seemed hopeless. A body of desperate men had formed the design of burning the barges, and commenced by setting fire to a raft composed of timbers soaked with oil and floating it down the river.

A groan of agony was sent forth from the unhappy wretches in the barges when this messenger of death was seen drifting towards them. Some of the men, driven to the verge of insanity by the suspense of the morning and the dread of death at any moment, proposed to desert the barges and try to swim to a place of safety. One of the captains put a quietus on the plan by threatening to blow out the brains of the first man who endeavored to desert his fellows in the face of danger which menaced all equally.

The burning raft failed to accomplish its mission. The flames which shot up from it when it was launched were gradually extinguished by the water and, by the time it reached the barges, it was only a charred and blackened mass.

Nowise discouraged by their failure, the men on shore turned their hand to a new plan of incendiarism. From the converting department of the mill down to the water's edge where the bargers were moored runs a railroad switch, forming a steep incline. A car was run on to this switch and loaded with barrels of oil, lumber, waste, and other combustibles. A torch was applied to the inflammable pile, and the car of fire, from which the flames mounted high in the air, was sent whirling down the incline. Thousands of eyes were fixed upon this spectacle. The Pinkertons gazed with blanched faces and trembling limbs, confident that their last hour had come. Far back on the hills, women and children watched what was being done and shouted their approval. The sharpshooters dropped their guns and looked on with bated breath.

Surely that fiery monster, looking like a thing of life as it sped downward, would crash into the barges and do its work with infernal effectiveness.

But no. Great as was the momentum of the car, it came to a sudden stop when the wheels embedded themselves in the soft soil at the water's edge, and the workmen were again baffled.

The Little Bill, which, in the absence of the wheelman, had been knocking about aimlessly between the barges and the shore, was the only sufferer. The little tug was badly scorched, and those on board had to labor like Trojans to preserve her from total destruction. After this crowning stroke of misfortune, Captain Rodgers decamped with all possible celerity, and went on down the river to Pittsburgh. His departure was a blow to the Pinkertons, who were hoping that the Little Bill might tow them out of danger. Now that the tug was gone, the last ray of hope vanished, and it seemed to be a question of only a short time until the expedition, already badly shattered, would be burnt up or blown up.

The Little Bill's departure was the signal for renewed firing, which was maintained so vigorously that probably not less than 1,000 shots were fired within ten minutes.

At this time the scenes in Homestead beggared description. The streets were filled with women, weeping, wailing and wringing their hands and begging for news of husband, sons and brothers. Females were excluded from the mill yard, and very wisely, for if admitted they would only have hampered the fighting men and exposed their own lives without benefit to anyone. In some places, substantial citizens gathered and discussed plans for stopping the conflict, the only drawback to which was that not one of them was feasible. Elsewhere groups of belligerents canvassed projects for the killing of the Pinkertons in a body. And all of this amid the crackling of rifle-shots and the din of a legion of angry voices.

DRAWING CONCLUSIONS

1. What were the underlying causes of the Homestead Strike?
2. What can we learn from the case of the Homestead Strike about the sources of conflict between workers and employers during the age of industrialization?

3.2 THE LOUISIANA SUGAR WAR OF 1887

Our second case is the Louisiana Sugar War of 1887 in which roughly 10,000 sugar plantation workers, primarily African American, went on strike against their employers. Prior to the Civil War, the sugar industry of southern Louisiana had depended upon the labor of enslaved workers. In the years after emancipation, newly freed sugar workers joined together and employed a variety of tactics to improve their conditions. These efforts reached their peak in 1887 when thousands of sugar workers joined the Knights of Labor and demanded that representatives of the sugar planters negotiate with them over wages for the coming season. Like the Homestead Strike, the 1887 sugar workers' strike ended in violence, with dozens of individuals (mainly striking workers and their supporters) left dead. As you read this account of the sugar workers' strike, look for common patterns with the Homestead Strike.

GUIDING QUESTIONS:

1. What specific issues were in dispute between sugar planters and the Knights of Labor?
2. Why weren't these issues resolved through compromise and negotiation?
3. What led to the violence between supporters of the sugar planters and striking workers in November 1887?

THE STRIKE OF 1887: LOUISIANA SUGAR WAR

BY JEFFREY GOULD

On November 1, 1887, Brigadier General William Pierce observed from his train the immediate effects of the most important strike in the history of rural Louisiana. An estimated 10,000 sugar plantation workers—most of whom were black, but 1,000 of whom were white—organized in the Knights of Labor (K of L), had stopped cutting and grinding sugarcane, in demand for wage increases and the abolition of scrip payments. Pierce reported that he saw "the fields in all directions full of cane, the mills idle, the stock and carts and wagons laid by and no work being done."

After more man three weeks of intense conflict, often involving General Pierce's, troops, this interracial class movement, degenerated into racial violence.

In the small city of Thibodaux, Louisiana, at dawn on November 23, 300 armed while vigilantes murdered over 50 black people. The Thibodaux Massacre ended the strike, fatally wounded the Labor movement, and initiated a racist reign of terror in the Louisiana sugar region.

. . .

PLANTERS AND THE LABOR QUESTION

In January 1874, less than a decade after slaves had deserted the sugar plantations en masse, black laborers along Black Bayou in Terrebonne Parish struck to resist wage cuts of 57 a month. Although the stale militia and neighboring Lafourche vigilantes repressed the movement after two weeks of struggle, this strike nevertheless influenced both the development of the labor movement in Lafourche and Terrebonne and planter strategy towards "the labor question."

. . .

Jeffrey Gould, "The Strike of 1877: Louisiana Sugar War," *Southern Exposure* 12 (November–December, 1984): 45–55.

The 1874 repression was but a Pyrrhic victory for the planters. Lafourche planters had demonstrated solidarity with their Terrebonne brothers, and the Republican state apparatus had rejected its black base to help put down the strike. But the political and economic organization of laborers, their generalized discontent with the wage system, and their aspirations for agrarian reform posed a continued threat to the planter class. During the next three years, laborers consistently sabotaged planter efforts to construct a wage system held together by force and designed to guarantee a labor supply permanently bound to plantations.

Workers resisted the planters in several ways. Typically, they moved at the end of the year and undermined the planters' class solidarity by inducing them to compete for labor. In addition, workers constantly resisted labor discipline. Since Emancipation, workers insisted on "doing things their own way." They occasionally enforced their own labor discipline by shooting uncooperative foremen. Finally, workers strove to convert their desire for agrarian reform into immediate reality. They devoted "excessive" time to their "arpents"—.85 acres of land ceded to each worker by the plants in order to diminish costs of supporting their labor. Particularly in lower Lafourche—which had a proportionately larger white and racially mixed population than the upper region—workers also acquired small plots of land to complement their fishing and trapping activities with subsistence farming and thereby escape the lot of permanent plantation laborers.

Labor resistance directly threatened the planters' prosperity, especially those "advanced" planters who were attempting to expand their operations and modernize their processing mills. Post-Reconstruction planters as a group were threatened by the development of a New York-based sugar trust which increasingly turned to cheap imports for its raw sugar. This trust further undermined the planters' economic power by producing a refined while sugar which by the mid-1880s was virtually the only type consumed in the U.S. The majority of Louisiana planters could only produce kettle-made brown sugars for sale to refineries. More than half of Louisiana's medium- and large-scale planters thus found themselves subject to the price dictates of the New York trust.

An emerging planter elite hoped to compete with the trust by developing their own highly mechanized sugar refineries. But to compete adequately, these "advanced" planter-manufacturers needed to process far more cane than they grew on their individual plantations; they had to expand their holdings or convert smaller planters, who were diverting a portion of their harvest to the making of molasses and brown sugar, into mere cane growers.

As we shall see, the evolving structural antagonism between elite and nonelite planters generated increasing tensions between "advanced" planters in various parts of the cane-growing parishes and the "backward" planters of other areas. It also fueled an anti-monopoly ideological discourse which conditioned the emergence of an interracial labor movement but which planters generally tried to turn to their advantage by focusing attention on the evils of the New York trust, New Orleans banks, and the railroads, which victimized the entire region.

From the elite planters' perspective, the development of local sugar refineries substantially minimized labor costs and dramatically increased the production of sugar per ton of cane by 50 percent during the 1870s and 1880s. But the production of cane was only slightly less labor-intensive than it had been during the ante-bellum period. Total labor costs for the production of refined sugar varied between one-half and two-thirds of the total business costs, with at least 75 percent of the wage bill devoted to agricultural labor. The efficient use and maximized productivity of field Labor was thus a fundamental, if not determinant, precondition for achieving the transition to a fully modern sugar industry under elite control. A free labor market, regulated by supply and demand, seemed to guarantee such a precondition.

The incipient planter class organization of 1873–74 failed to halt labor unrest or to establish itself on a permanent basis. In 1877 Donelson Caffery, an elite St. Mary's planter (and later U.S. senator) issued the following call for planter unity:

There are occurrences of recent date and ills of long standing which required prompt and combined action on the part of the planters of St. Mary. Quite recently a deliberate attempt was made to burn down in one night four large sugar houses. . . . The labor question is also very serious. The destruction consequent upon the ruinous policy of competition among the planters, though not so immediate, is considerably surer than by fire. We may guard against the attempts of the incendiary, but how as to curbing our appetite for our neighbor's servant? We can observe the laws of supply and demand. A serious question for them [the planters] to consider is the matter of strikes. From the monthly payment of wages in full and the execrable system of job work largely obtaining all over the parish, the labor has been spasmodic, unreliable and [discontent] on the rise this whole season. . . .

The New Orleans *Daily Picayune* firmly supported Caffery's position, calling the labor question "the most important subject to be considered . . . at this time." In October, a month after Caffery's call, the Louisiana Sugar Planters Associations (LSPA) fanned and proposed a program which would modify the free market wage system in order to ensure a successful transition to modem industry. First, the planter elite, as we have seen, proposed to unify wage scales, thus eliminating planter competition for laborers. Second, they sought to establish a uniform wage withholding system. Eighty percent of the wages would be withheld monthly. On large plantations, scrip payments coerced workers into buying commodities at company stores. These stores sometimes charged 100 percent more than market prices. The scrip and wage withholding system fostered laborer indebtedness, which in turn guaranteed a dependent labor supply.

Third, planters struggled to supplant the "job system," whereby a laborer would contract for a specific job such as hoeing, ploughing, woodchopping, or ditch-digging. Laborers strongly preferred this system, but planters, not surprisingly, found it incompatible with the military-like discipline necessary to run a modernizing sugar plantation.

Finally, planters attempted gradually to replace black male laborers with a cheaper and more docile labor force. Depending on the demographic and geographic characteristics of the region, planters proposed white immigration or the use of female black labor as a way of eliminating "undesirable" black male labor. Since Emancipation, black women had withdrawn themselves from the permanent plantation labor force, but in the late 1870s and 1880s planters strove to re-integrate them. By 1887 elite planters had created a sexual division of labor wherein female labor often exclusively planted and cut the cane. Planters paid women 25 to 40 percent less than males for the same work. The strategic creation of a sexual division of labor to complement the racial division not only created another cleavage in the work force but also tended to depress wage levels in general. Planters assumed that they were supplanting "unreliable" with "docile" labor. . . .

From 1877 through 1887 laborers struggled intensely against the implementation of the LSPA program. In 1880 workers in five parishes along the Mississippi River struck in demand of 50 percent wage increases. The relatively mild repression of these movements, which involved hundreds of workers in each locality, in no way dampened the spirit of black proletarian resistance. Not a grinding season passed between 1881 and 1886 without reports of strikes in the sugar region. In October 1886 a strike of 250 cane cutters in Plaquemines announced another harvest of discontent. In January 1887, in upper Lafourche, 15 allegedly armed blacks organized a strike on three major plantations. A sheriff's posse apprehended eight of the militants. The *Thibodaux Sentinel* commented on the incident: "Un signe des temps."

Strikes and strike threats were not the only means of worker resistance in the 1880s. The daily struggle against labor discipline—in the case of elite plantations, the militaristic control over the labor process in the fields—was intense and violent. In 1880 a planter in St. Mary's underscored the gravity of these struggles:

"They [blacks] are becoming more and more unmanageable. By degree they are bringing the planter to their way of thinking in regard to how they should work and no ceiling at what moment there will be a serious move to compel the planter to comply with any request. . . ."

Foremen killed workers occasionally in order to set a disciplinary example. Similarly, foremen were the immediate target of the workers' resistance to discipline. On November 16, 1880, for example, an assistant overseer murdered a laborer in the fields. On January 30, 1886, to cite one of numerous cases, laborer Albert Williams killed the overseer on W.H. Minor's Southdown Plantation in Terrebonne with a hoe. Revolvers proved a more common method of fighting the daily class war in the fields. The *Sentinel* commented succinctly, "Notre contre [sic] est toujours la terre classique du revolver." (Our wars are always fought with revolvers.)

From 1874 to 1887, in a largely unorganized fashion, workers fought against militarized discipline and economic coercion, and for above-subsistence wages. When the laborers organized themselves into the K of L, their tactical goals synthesized previous struggles and threatened the very core of the elite planters' transitional program towards a "modern sugar industry." First, the organization of the K of L amounted to a formalized counterpower in the fields and mills. Second, organized workers demanded the elimination of the mechanisms which the planter considered essential to maintain a stable, dependent, and docile labor force. The workers demanded that payments in scrip instead of cash be abolished, that cash payments be made at short intervals rather than withheld for long periods, and that wages be increased to above subsistence levels. Their further demand for a unified wage category—$1.25 a day and $.60 a night for all workers—directly subverted planter efforts to depress the wages of male laborers, if not to replace them completely with lower-paid female workers. Finally, the cooperativist and anti-monopolist ideology of K of L militants threatened the planter elite's hegemony in land ownership.

THE KNIGHTS ORGANIZE

Inspired by national railroad strikes organized or supported by the K of L, white railroad workers in Morgan City organized the first local assembly in the sugar region in the fall of *1885.* The role these workers played in the February 1886 New Orleans-organized strike on the Morgan Line is unclear, but it was at that moment that they surfaced publicly. On February 22, 1886, the Morgan City *Free Press* greeted this development:

The *Free Press* notes with pleasure the organization of the laborers of Morgan City; it is something that should have been done years ago, for in no locality has labor been more imposed upon than here. Every effort has been made by the railroad monopoly to destroy the independence of its employees. They were not expected to have opinions of their own. If the Morgan Line considered that a certain storekeeper was unfriendly, the employees were given to understand that he was not to receive their trade, and woe be to him who failed to understand. . . . We would advise every laborer to join the association . . . to insist that the laborer is to work so many hours, to receive so much money and to spend that money when and where he pleases.

The unique conditions of this company town (population 2,500) organized around Charles Morgan's Railroad and Steamship Company provided fertile ground for the K of L organization. By July 1886 black railroad workers had organized a 150-member local which acted in concert with the white local. Within a year a total of seven locals, ranging from 50 to 150 members and including clothing and domestic workers, were functioning in the Morgan City area. At least 80 percent of the work force belonged to the K of L. This precocious organizational development would have profound consequences for the labor movement in the sugar region.

The concentration of district leadership in the hands of white railroad workers spurred the development of the K of L along the railroad lines; however, outside of its connection through railroads and steamboats, K of L district leadership was isolated from its base in the plantation zones of St. Mary's, Terrebonne, and Lafourche parishes. Moreover, the railroad-based organizational network tended to preclude the unification into the Knights local organization, District Assembly (DA) 194, of such parishes as St. James, St. John the Baptist, and St. Charles, which were areas of intense strike activity in 1880. Thus thousands of potential militants were excluded from DA 194, and from any role in the 1887 strike.

The K of L domination of Morgan City also had direct political consequences. Anti-monopolism, as typified by the *Free Press* editorial, was an ideological perspective which appealed to nearly the entire population. In politics and economics, specific conditions supported an interclass alliance, which middle-class elements dominated. The municipal elections of January 1887 resulted in a sweep for K of L candidates. Four out of five of the elected officers were white merchants and physicians. This election served as a model for similar interclass district assembly organizations in Franklin and in the Lafourche Parish seat of Thibodaux.

Small planters, farmers, urban workers, artisans, and small merchants all suffered at the hands of banks and railroad monopolies. Anti-monopolism oriented these social groups for self-defense against financial, commercial, and transportation interests which threatened to submerge them in a sea of foreclosures, bankruptcy, unemployment, and inflation. For the elite planters, the New York "Trust," New Orleans banks, and sugar factors (agents) provided a clear focus for development of an anti-monopolist discourse which could unify, under elite control, distinct social groups in the sugar region. But such a cohesive ideology was rendered problematic by the very monopolistic tendencies inherent in the elite planters' movement toward centralizing the local manufacturing process and dominating the primary producers. Trapped between a nascent anti-monopolist alliance on the one side and continual plantation laborer unrest on the other, the planter elite in the 1880s had to make important ideological and political concessions to the alliance. But these very concessions on the one flank would debilitate elite defenses against labor.

Anti-monopolism as championed by the Knights of Labor in the countryside had two concrete meanings for laborers. First, it meant resistance to those aspects of plantation wage labor which coerced them into remaining under planter domination: subsistence wages, scrip payment, and wage withholdings. Second, the K of L prescription for a new system based on cooperative production meshed perfectly with traditional desires for agrarian reform.

The Knights program attracted skilled workers, laborers, shop owners, several white newspaper editors, and black schoolteachers involved in the local Republican Party which opposed plantation domination of politics. On August 12, 1886, the first local

assembly of sugar workers was organized in the town of Schriever, which was little more than a railroad depot located in the midst of the most productive and modernized sector of the Terrebonne sugar industry. A year later, LA 8404 had over 300 members. Originally composed exclusively of black workers, it grew to become the first integrated branch of the K of L, and it is probable that this local initiated the plans to make wage demands on the Planters Association in 1887.

Other locals sprang up throughout the sugar region, in both the upper "advanced" and lower "backward" areas: some were segregated by race and trade, others were mixed, and most were exclusively dominated by male middle-class and working-class leaders.

THE STRIKE

In August 1887 the leaders of DA 194 proposed negotiations with the St. Mary's branch of the LSPA, citing the universal predictions of a bumper crop and expressing the desire to avoid a "misunderstanding" between employer and employee. The LSPA politely refused the proposed negotiations. At that moment, the DA 194 leadership sought to increase its leverage by incorporating Terrebonne and Lafourche assemblies into its radius of action. Constant communication about organizational growth, brief work stoppages, and economic distress undoubtedly conditioned this decision. At the time, the leadership did not anticipate the necessity of engaging in strike activity to obtain wage increases and the abolition of the scrip system. Nevertheless, they felt that if necessary a strike would triumph, given the solidarity of railroad and steamboat workers who would block attempts to bring in scabs (probably convict laborers).

Curiously, K of L leaders did not anticipate the use of the state militia to protect strikebreakers. The union had several militant members in the militia, and the railroad men may have supposed that because the militia consisted of $2.50-a-day "mechanics" like themselves, class solidarity would prevail. Although several white railroad workers had conquered their own racism to the point of being tireless organizers of black workers, the K of L also failed to recognize that other white workers were not as committed to the Knight's doctrine of interracial solidarity. Nor did the K of L see the weakness in allowing middle-class merchants, craftsmen, and professionals to take positions of leadership over a working-class agenda. Indeed, as St. Mary's planters met during October to devise strike-breaking tactics, they received the collaboration of the white middle-class-dominated assembly in Franklin.

The full extent of the internal weaknesses of the Knights had not yet emerged, and on October 19 delegates from DA 194's three parishes met and in a militant mood adopted three demands:

1. wage increases from $1 to $1.25 per 12-hour day shift and from $.50 to $.60 for the six-hour night shift ("watch");
2. elimination of scrip;
3. payment every two weeks for the day shift and every week for obligatory night work.

The delegates resolved to strike on November 1 if the planters did not agree to their demands. K of L leaders in Lafourche let it be known that they would compromise if the demands were considered "exorbitant." The planters in Thibodaux, on the other hand, left no doubt about their position. Comforted by the knowledge that 11 artillery companies and two cavalry detachments were ready to occupy the sugar district, Republican judge Taylor Beattie and Democratic state senator E.A. O'Sullivan, in a nonpartisan gesture, organized a meeting of planters on Saturday, October 30. The planters and other "influential people" refused to recognize the K of L or any of its demands, pledged to blacklist any discharged employees, and promised the lawful eviction of any strikers on the plantation.

Lafourche planters awoke the next morning to find that virtually no laborers had reported to work. Planter morale, however, was uplifted by the 4:00 p.m. arrival at the train depot: of two companies of the state militia composed of 48 men equipped with a Gatling gun, which they installed in front of the courthouse. A crowd of 500 black and white strikers peaceably gathered in the town square facing the troops and their Gatling gun. Inside the courthouse, Judge Beattie presided over a hastily called meeting of planters from the Thibodaux area.

Beattie and the planters briefed the militia's Brigadier General Pierce on the situation in Lafourche. The strike was practically general throughout the parish, Planters in lower Lafourche had already given in to the strikers' demands, selling a precedent which threatened planter solidarity. Moreover, bringing in strikebreakers to upper Lafourche would prove difficult. Already the laborers had refused to vacate their cabins when ordered to do so by the planters. General Pierce listened patiently, and then strongly suggested that the strikers had to be evicted immediately. Judge Beattie and Judge Knoblock (an ex-planter who was both a district judge and lieutenant governor) issued warrants for the arrest of over a dozen strikers. The planters promised to defray all state expenses and to board and lodge all militiamen.

On Wednesday, November 2, the situation in Thibodaux became more strained as evicted strikers from neighboring plantations moved their possessions into the black and mulatto areas of town. A sheriff's posse supported by State troops arrested several workers who refused to vacate their cabins. Local K of L leaders posted bond and obtained their release.

Late in the afternoon, General Pierce met with Judge Beattie and Lieutenant·Governor Knoblock. Beattie and Knoblock believed the Strike would be settled in "two or three days, but the General was impatient." He urged the militia to commence "heroic and vigorous action" to enforce the eviction of all strikers (the majority still remained) from their plantation-owned homes. As if sent by fate to win the general's argument, C.S. Mathews, a prosperous Lockport planter, burst into the courthouse and declared that in lower Lafourche "scenes of depredations and bloodshed were imminent" on both sides of the bayou in the Lockport area. He asked for a company of militia to go to the region, inaccessible by rail or telegraph. On Thursday, one militia battalion journeyed by train to Raceland and then made the seven-mile march to the Mathews place.

In Thibodaux, the K of L local leadership foresaw the mounting problems caused by the state's armed presence and control of the railroads: they would have to sustain and discipline an increasing Thibodaux population of evicted strikers. Negotiations for goals short of total victory were thus imperative, and were apparently going on with Beattie's group of elite planters. Indeed, on the third day of the strike, a negotiated settlement seemed a distinct possibility. However, the news that planter Rochard Forel had been shot on his Lockport plantation in self-defense by a K of L militant, Moses Pugh, aborted the possibility of a negotiated settlement.

Accompanied by a deputy sheriff's posse, General Pierce made a four-and-a-half-hour journey by buggy from Thibodaux to Lockport. When the general arrived, he found Foret's condition satisfactory. A large crowd of blacks "hooted and used violent language, the women waving shirts on poles, and jeering," when the battalion arrested Pugh. K of L delegates Gustave Antoine and Julius Allen were also arrested on charges of obstructing justice. Three black small farmers—the Goff brothers and Henry Franklin—posted bail.

The violence in Lockport, in southern Lafourche, undoubtedly hardened Pierce's militancy. The Lafourche Planters' Association met the next day, on Saturday, November 4, to assess the situation which seemed to be shifting in their favor. In upper Lafourche perhaps 20 percent of the labor force (mostly women) had returned that morning to work, hungry and intimidated by the troops. The planters organized massive shipments of strikebreakers from the now terminated cotton harvests in Mississippi. Moreover, they had succeeded in driving a wedge through the K of L leadership in Thibodaux. When Delphin Monnier, a white small farmer and K of L delegate, was beaten for protesting the arrests of two fellow white strikers in Laurel Valley, he switched sides from being a "dangerous anarchist" to join L.c. Aubert, the K of L building contractor, in a public condemnation of the strike. Given these favorable developments, the planters believed, negotiations with the strikers had lost their urgency. The association lodged a formal request with General Pierce to maintain the state forces in Thibodaux until the strikebreakers were safely at work.

Events in St. Mary's further augmented the Lafourche planters' power. Military occupation of the railroads effectively isolated the DA 194 leadership in Morgan City. Pattersonville, a predominantly black town, became the focus of strike activity during the first week of November, as hundreds of evicted strikers moved there. On November 5, a sheriff's posse led by K of L white delegate A.J. Frere and supported by a battalion of state militia marched into the town and massacred between five and 20 residents. Donelson Caffery, the elite planter who had issued the call for planter unity a decade earlier, described himself as a reluctant participant in the massacre, and a week later wrote:

I think I will make 3 or 4 thousand if I can save my crop. The strike is effectually squelched. It was necessary to apply a strong remedy. The negroes are quiet and with few exceptions have gone to work. A few bad white men ought to be harshly dealt with and then there will be no more.

One black K of L leader wrote during that fateful week: "The planters and Government are trying to crush our Order out of existence . . . But they only strengthen our resolve." Nevertheless, this labor militant substantiated Caffery's and newspaper assertions that the Mary's strike movement was mortally weakened by the racist violence. He ended his letter by stating that his 377-member black local had leased a large plantation which they planned to work as a cooperative, thus indicating he recognized that a strike victory was unlikely.

The weakening of the strike movement in Terrebonne Parish further isolated Lafourche workers from any potential solidarity. The Terrebonne workers struck one week earlier than the Lafourche laborers; elite planters there placed orders for Mississippi white and black strikebreakers, and by November 10, 800 were working the Terrebonne plantation. State militia aggressively protected the welfare of the strikebreakers. Local authorities, backed by militia, arrested at least 50 strikers in a "modern" section of Terrebonne. In the rest of the parish at least 11 of the less prominent planters, in zones where whites formed a significant part of the work force, had acceded to the strike demands. A visit from a national K of L organizer and the continued support of the Terrebonne *Times* apparently stimulated a second wave of strike activity in the Houma-Schreiver area between November 15 and 20. During this period, a militant laborer wrote from Terrebonne:

The cane being ripe, the planters must either come to terms or lose their crops. The many companies of the stale militia cannot harvest the crops nor drive the united laborers to do so at starvation prices.

By November 20, however, the strike had ended in the modern sector of Terrebonne. The militia and planter-organized vigilante committee guaranteed the right to work for strikebreakers And demoralized laborers. The plantations where the strikers had triumphed had no practical effect on the parish's sugar plantations as a whole. The black and white workers of Canal Belanger, a "backward" zone, maintained the only pocket of resistance, but they were by November 20 alone and cut off from all communications.

The failure of the strike in St. Mary's and Terrebonne, at the very least, made it clear to upper Lafourche K of L militants that they would have to continue the fight alone. Moreover, since the first week of November the DA 194 leadership had not communicated with Lafourche militants. New Orleans DA 102's gesture of solidarity—a blistering condemnation of Governor McEnery's military intervention in general and the Pattersonville massacre in particular, as well as an appeal to the nation's working class to work for the repeal of the sugar tariff to "bring the planters to a sense of justice"—had served only to strengthen the planters' position. Elite planters who backed McEnery's opponent in the December Democratic primary could not help but close ranks with the other planters in support of the governor and his military agent, General Pierce. Republican Judge Beattie of course was thrilled that the troops had named their site "Camp Beattie," and the K of L manifesto had snapped the last bond of sympathy he may have felt towards his former black Republican allies. Moreover, the white population of Thibodaux, including many former K of L supporters, seemed to be turning against the strikers. After all, a repeal of the sugar tariff would destroy the town more thoroughly than the newly circulating rumor of a plot by black strikers to burn the town.

Although the Thibodaux K of L leaders protested that they maintained a strict discipline in Thibodaux and that no violence had occurred since the strike began, they could not deny that unknown people had shot into several sugar mills in upper Lafourche, where small groups of local white workers processed the cane cut by the reduced crew of strikebreakers.

The foreman on the Leighton place was wounded the night of November 16. On November 17, Judge Beanie, accompanied by a small armed entourage of local residents, walked into the K of L's office in the St. Charles Street area. His visit was brief. He did not wish to talk, and stated only that "the shooting and burning must cease. You will be personally held responsible . . . the community must begin to look to their lives and property and protect themselves." The committee left before the K of L leaders could protest their innocence. Beanie and his group went back to the Hotel de Ville and began a very serious discussion.

The Thibodaux-area planters were truly amazed at the determination and resourcefulness of the strikers. Not one of the more than 500 newcomers was having to sleep outdoors. Somehow the newcomers were bringing in food to the strikers, probably with the help of black farmers from the Lockport area. (Down there the strike was basically over. The planters had given in, with the exception of Mathews, who was allowed to work half a crew unmolested. The old eccentric planter Godchaux had his force back at work on the strikers' terms. He was getting richer every day, a bad precedent for planter unity.) Beattie admitted that the general had assessed the situation correctly at every juncture. Pierce had indeed been right to force the eviction issue with "heroic and vigorous" action. But this had worked better in Terrebonne where the planters had not counted on an early settlement and had brought in a sufficient quantity of strikebreakers. In the Thibodaux area, two Laurel Valley planters had already lost half of their crops and the weather was getting colder; a freeze would wreak more damage and the Thibodaux strikers showed no signs of weakening. Even the "arrogance" of the local black women—mostly their own domestic workers—was beginning to grate on the planters. The general had long argued that the planters take bolder steps on their own and in the last few days he suggested that "the troops were . . . in the road of an early settlement of the strike." Now the committee accepted his argument for local-based repression. They petitioned him to maintain the Shreveport Guards in town until Monday, November 21. By then the planters would have organized their "self-defense."

On Sunday afternoon, November 20, Rhody DeZauche, the barrel maker, was giving a speech to a large group of black strikers on the south side of tile Thibodaux canal. A sheriff's posse grouped on the other side of the canal. The sheriff thought he heard DeZauche call for the burning of Thibodaux, and the predominantly black crowd responded with loud cheers. The heavily armed white men crossed the bridge and grabbed DeZauche. The sheriff arrested him on charges of conspiracy to commit murder.

Mary Pugh, the adult daughter of a prominent planter family from Assumption parish, wrote to her son that she was wondering aloud, as she walked out of church, if the congregation would be allowed to celebrate Thanksgiving. News from the canal interrupted her meditation. Many armed whites raced towards the south side. As she started walking home, she became terrified by the spectacle of three black men walking down the other side of the street, armed with double-barreled shot guns. A black woman leaned out a window and shouted: "Fight yes! Fight! We'll be there."

On Sunday evening a crowd of 300 white men gathered to hear speeches by town officials and elite planters. They were urged to constitute themselves as a local militia, deputized to guard every "entrance and inlet" to the town. The speakers claimed that there were strong indications that blacks planned to invade Thibodaux, aided by the strikers who had stockpiled arms on St. Charles Street. From Sunday night until Wednesday at dawn, over 300 "pickets,"—Thibodaux residents and white volunteers from neighboring parishes thoroughly guarded the town day and night. No black person could enter or leave the town without the written permission of Judge Beattie.

Monday morning two K of L delegates went to see the mayor. They protested vehemently that rumors of impending black violence were totally unfounded, and that the few arms in black hands were shotguns for self-defense. They urged the reopening of negotiations.

On Monday night a group of armed white men walked into Henry Franklin's crowded barroom. Two shots exploded. Two black men staggered out of the bar onto Jackson Street. One fell down. The other walked for a block and dropped dead.

Tuesday morning the planters announced that they were engaged in fruitful negotiations with the strikers. K of L leaders Henry and George Cox were then arrested on charges of making incendiary speeches. Later, Beattie would call the charges misdemeanors. Throughout the night, vigilantes rode through the St. Charles area shooting into the air.

Between 4:00 and 5:00 a.m. Wednesday morning, Joseph Molaison, the son of a dry goods store owner, and Henry Donnan, a co-proprietor of a foundry, were warming their freezing hands over a fire by a "picket" station on St. Charles Street. Unidentified people, most probably blacks trying to escape from Thibodaux, fired two shots. One bullet grazed Molaison's leg. Another bullet entered Gorman's head, just below his bushy eyebrows. Miraculously the bullet emerged out of his bloody mouth. The shots snapped groggy deputies to attention. The impulse for retribution propelled them from Beattie's courthouse to St. Charles Street, where pickets were already storming a large brick building which housed many strikers' families.

Every shot which pierced the cold dawn air made Mary Pugh thankful that her husband had left town. She saw crowds of armed white men leading blacks along with the English carpenter Foote, a K of L leader, towards the commons. Then the noise became deafening, like that of a battle.

She looked across the canal and saw elite planter Andrew Price lead a group of men into a house. They emerged dragging a black man with them. The group crossed the bridge over the canal and walked right past Mary Pugh's side gate. She, along with a few neighbors, followed. She thought they were headed to the jail, but:

Instead they walked with one over to the lumber yard where they told him to "run for his life"—gave the order to fire—all raised their rifles and shot him dead. This was the worst sight I saw, but I tell you we have had a horrible three days and Wednesday excelled anything I ever saw even during the War. I am sick—with the horror of it—but I know it had to be else we would have been murdered before a great while—I think this will settle the question of who is to rule the nigger or the white man for the next fifty years.

AFTERMATH

Mary Pugh estimated over 50 Black people were massacred on the morning of November 23, 1887. Others estimated the death toll at from 30 to 300. Judge Beattie released the Cox brothers from prison later that morning and told them to run for their lives. Solomon Williams sought official protection, but instead was marched to the bayou. All three K of L leaders were most likely assassinated. Ten months later a band of white vigilantes—a common sight in post-November Lafourche—broke into Gustave Antoine's house, dragged him to a tree, tied him up, and riddled his body with bullets. Earlier in the year a similar group "expropriated" the black farming co-operative in Antoine's neighborhood.

In Terrebonne, the end of the strike initiated a period of terror principally against black people. "Regulators" drove most militants from the parish. The editor of the Terrebonne *Times*, Dr. H. M. Wallis, a K of L supporter in Houma, wrote:

The record of crime growing out of our labor trouble is now complete, blood has been shed and the moloch of vengeance has been satiated with the sacrifice of human life. And who is to blame for this state of affairs? We answer unhesitatingly the intelligent though not over scrupulous planter. In his bullheadedness he has over shot the mark and is answerable for his recklessness. Either through his inspiration or disloyalty to the mandates of the civil law and the rights of others, there has sprung into the existence a mushroom crop of bull-dozers all over the troubled section, who arc exercising unauthorized vengeance upon the unarmed negroes—such a sight sickens sympathy and destroys all regard for law. . . . The object of these intimidators seems to be

twofold; first to break up the lodges of the Knights of Labor and scatter its membership, and secondly to make use of intimidation for political effect.

Only two K of L assemblies functioned in Lafourche and Terrebonne Parishes in November 1888. These were LA 1043 at Canal Belanger and LA 10943 at Harangville, precisely the less technologically advanced and racially more open zones where the K of L had won at least partial victories.

On February 21, 1888, Donelson Caffery, the elite planter and politician, wrote to his wife: "I went to Pattersonville on Sunday and organized a branch of the 'law and order league.' They are very enthusiastic down there to have a white man's government." Caffery, along with other "progressive" planters, had at last found a political solution to the "labor question" which had plagued them throughout the decade. The smashing of the labor movement and the establishment of racist political rule in the region shaped the transition to modem industry.

The immediate effect of the union defeat on Lafourche and Terrebonne laborers, beyond generalized terrorism, is hard to ascertain. Reports from neighboring parishes, however, make it clear that the planter elite used their consolidated power to solidify mechanisms designed to maintain a submissive and stable work force. By September 1888 scrip payments equivalent to subsistence wages prevailed throughout the region. A laborer in St. John's wrote: "If members of a family be more than two it costs more for living than the present wages can afford." In addition, in many cases planters began to charge rent for cabins and to deny laborers' right to farm an *arpent*. Thus as the elite tied laborers to the plantations through scrip they turned into monetary terms every social relationship within their domain, thereby further deepening the workers' dependency and bondage through indebtedness.

By 1894 over half of the sugar mills operating in 1887 had ceased to grind cane. Former small manufacturers became cane farmers, supplying the elite central factories. During the same brief period sugar production increased over 100 percent. By 1900 the organization of production in the sugar region only vaguely resembled the system prevalent in the 1880s:

production was almost entirely concentrated in a handful of fully modernized central factories, operated almost exclusively by white labor. On the greatly expanded elite plantations in the leading sugar parishes of St. Mary's, Terrebonne, and Lafourche, many new white tenants closely supervised small groups of black laborers (often female), who worked in the fields from dawn to dusk, under conditions approximating slavery.

DRAWING CONCLUSIONS:

1. What were the underlying causes of the Louisiana Sugar War?
2. What can we learn from the case of the Louisiana Sugar War about the sources of conflict between workers and employers during the age of industrialization?

3.3 THE NEW YORK CITY KOSHER MEAT BOYCOTT OF 1902

The social conflicts of the age of industrialization took many forms, among the most interesting of which were food riots in which working-class consumers (primarily women) violently protested increases in food prices. (Keep in mind that the general trend in consumer prices was downward during the age of industrialization.) One example of such protest was a meat boycott waged by Jewish immigrant women in New York City in 1902. As you read historian Paula Hyman's account of the boycott, ask yourself why this protest campaign (like the Homestead Strike) resulted in violence. One thing to keep in mind is that due to Jewish dietary practices, religiously observant Jews could only buy meat from a limited number of butchers whose products had been certified as "kosher."

GUIDING QUESTIONS:

1. What motivated the women who led the Kosher Meat Boycott of 1902?
2. Why did the boycott result in violence?

IMMIGRANT WOMEN AND CONSUMER PROTEST

THE NEW YORK CITY KOSHER MEAT BOYCOTT OF 1902 PAULA E. HYMAN

Women have always participated in politics. Despite their eclipse in the conventional seats of political power, women in preindustrial societies frequently engaged in popular protest, particularly when the price, or availability, of basic foodstuffs was at issue. As one English historian of the working class and of popular culture has pointed out regarding eighteenth century food riots, women were "those most involved in face-to-face marketing [and hence] most sensitive to price significancies. . . ." In fact, he adds, "it is probable that the women most frequently precipitated the spontaneous actions." In the popular ferment of the early days of the French Revolution, women were also conspicuous by their presence. The image of grim-faced market women on the march to Versailles to bring the royal family back to Paris has been sharply etched in the mind of every student of history or enthusiast of historical dramas. Even before the emergence of modern political movements committed to the recruitment of women into the political process, the "crowd" was an important means of self-pression for women's economic and political interests.

Immigrant Jewish women, too, took to the streets in spontaneous food riots on several occasions. Like their British and French forerunners more than a century before, they were reacting to the sharp rise in the price of food. Most noted and flamboyant of these incidents were the 1902 kosher meat riots in New York City. Erupting in mid-May, they precipitated political activity which continued for almost a month, attracting considerable attention both within the Jewish community and the larger urban society. Indeed, in a fierce and vitriolic editorial of May 24, 1902, the *New York Times* called for a speedy and determined police repression of this "dangerous class . . . especially

From Hyman, Paula E. "Immigrant Women and Consumer Protest: The New York City Kosher Meat Boycott of 1902." *American Jewish History* 70 (September 1980) 91–100.

the women [who] are very ignorant [and] . . . mostly speak a foreign language . . . It will not do," the editorial continued, "to have a swarm of ignorant and infuriated women going about any part of this city with petroleum destroying goods and trying to set fire to the shops of those against whom they are angry."

What impelled immigrant Jewish housewives to take to the streets (of Williamsburg, in this case) with bottles of kerosene in their hands? Was this simply an act of spontaneous rage, a corroboration of the English writer Robert Southey's comment that "women are more disposed to be mutinous [than men.]" Are the kosher meat riots a late manifestation, as Herbert Gutman has suggested, of a pre-industrial sensibility that focused upon the illegitimacy of violating a fair price for food? Finally, and most importantly, what can we learn of the self-perceptions, political consciousness, and sense of community of immigrant Jewish women by examining their role in this incident?

Despite their superficial similarity to earlier food riots, the kosher meat riots of 1902 give evidence of a modern and sophisticated political mentality emerging in a rapidly changing community. With this issue of the high price of food, immigrant housewives found a vehicle for political organization. They articulated a rudimentary grasp of their power as consumers and domestic managers. And, combining both traditional and modern tactics, they temporarily turned their status as housewives to good advantage, and used the neighborhood network to stage a successful three-week boycott of kosher meat shops throughout the Lower East Side, parts of upper Manhattan and The Bronx, and Brooklyn. The dynamics of the kosher meal boycott suggest that by focusing almost exclusively upon organized political activity in the labor movement and the socialist parties, historians have overlooked the role of women. Although for a great part of their life absent from the wage-earning market, immigrant Jewish women were not apolitical. They simply expressed their political concerns in a different, less historically accessible arena—the neighborhood—where they pioneered in local community organizing.

In early May, 1902, the retail price of kosher meat had soared from twelve cents to eighteen cents

a pound. Small retail butchers, concerned that their customers would not be able to afford their produce, refused to sell meat for a week to pressure the wholesalers (commonly referred to as the Meat Trust) to lower their prices. When their May 14th settlement with the wholesalers brought no reduction in the retail price of meat, Lower East Side housewives, milling in the street, began to call for a strike against the butchers. As one activist, Mrs. Levy, the wife of a cloakmaker, shouted, "This is their strike? Look at the good it has brought! Now, if *we women* make a Strike, then it will be a strike." Gathering support on the block—Monroe Street and Pike Street—Mrs. Levy and Sarah Edelson, owner of a small restaurant, called a mass meeting to spread the word of the planned boycott.

The next day, after a neighborhood canvas staged by the organizing committee, thousands of women streamed through the streets of the Lower East Side. breaking into butcher shops, flinging meat into the streets, and declaring a boycott. "Women were the ringleaders at all hours," noted the *New York Herold.* Customers who tried to carry their purchased meat from the butcher shops were forced to drop it. One woman emerging from a butcher store with meat for her sick husband was vociferously chided by an elderly woman wearing the traditional sheitel that "a sick man can eat tref meat." Within half an hour, the *Forward* reported, the strike had spread from one block through the entire area. Twenty thousand people were reported to have massed in front of the New Irving Hall. "Women were pushed and hustled about [by the police]. thrown to the pavement . . . and trampled upon," wrote the *Herald.* One policeman, trying to rescue those buying meat, had "an unpleasant moist piece of liver slapped in his face." Patrol wagons filled the streets, hauling women, some bleeding from their encounters with the police, into court. About seventy women and fifteen men were arrested on charges of disorderly conduct.

After the first day of street rioting, a mass meeting to rally support and map strategy was held at the initiative of the women activists, who had formed a committee. Two of their number addressed the crowd, as did the popular figure Joseph Barondess and the Zionist leader Rabbi Zeft. The next day, May

16, Lower East Side women again went from house to house to strengthen the boycott. Individuals were urged not to enter butcher shops or purchase meat. Pickets were appointed to stand in front of each butcher shop. On each block funds were collected to pay the fines of those arrested and to reimburse those customers whose meat had been confiscated in the first day of rioting. The *Tribune* reported that "an excitable and aroused crowd roamed the streets . . . As was the case on the previous day, the main disturbance was caused by the women. Armed with sticks, vocabularies and well sharpened nails, they made life miserable for the policemen." On the second day of rioting another hundred people were arrested." The boycott also spread, under local leadership, to the Bronx and to Harlem, where a mass meeting was held at Central Hall.

On Saturday, May 17th, the women leaders of the boycott continued their efforts, going from synagogue to synagogue to agitate on behalf of the boycott. Using the traditional communal tactic of interrupting the Torah reading when a matter of justice was at stake, they called on the men in each congregation to encourage their wives not to buy meat and sought rabbinic endorsement of their efforts. For once, urged a boycott leader, citing a Biblical passage, let the men use the power of "And he shall rule over her" to the good by seeing to it that their wives refrain from purchasing meat.

By Sunday, May 18th, most butcher shops on the Lower East Side bowed to reality and closed their doors. And the boycott had spread to Brooklyn, where the store windows of open butcher shops had been broken and meat burned. That night, the women held another meeting, attended by more than five hundred persons, to consolidate their organization, now named the Ladies' Anti-Beef Trust Association. Under the presidency of Mrs. Caroline Schatzburg, it proposed to continue house-to-house patrols, keep watch over butcher stores, and begin agitating for similar action among Christian women. Circulars bearing a skull and crossbones and the slogan "Eat no meat while the Trust is taking meat from the bones of your women and children" were distributed throughout the Jewish quarters of the city. The Association established six similar committees

to consolidate the boycott in Brownsville, East New York, and the Bronx. Other committees were set up to visit the labor and benevolent societies, labor union meetings, and lodges and to plan the establishment of cooperative stores. The Association also sent a delegation to the mayor's office to seek permission for an open air rally. Local groups of women continued to enforce the boycott in their neighborhoods. In Brooklyn four hundred women signed up to patrol neighborhood butcher stores. Buyers of meat continued to be assaulted and butcher shop windows smashed. In Harlem two women were arrested when they lay down on the elevated tracks to prevent a local butcher from heading downtown with meat for sale. Throughout the city's Jewish neighborhoods restaurants had ceased serving meat.

However, competition between Sarah Edelson, one of the founders of the boycott, and Caroline Schatzburg, the president of the Ladies' Anti-Beef Trust Association, erupted by May 18th into open quarrels between their followers at meetings. Taking advantage of this rivalry and winning the support of Edelson and her backers, on May 21st male communal leaders, with David Blaustein of the Educational Alliance presiding, held a conference of three hundred representatives of synagogues, *hevras*, landsmanshaften, and unions "to bring order to the great struggle for cheap meat." In his remarks at the conference meeting, Joseph Barondess made explicit that a new leadership was asserting itself. Urging the women to be quiet and leave the fighting to the men, he noted that otherwise the women would be held responsible in the event of the boycott's defeat. Calling themselves the Allied Conference for Cheap Kosher Meat, the male conference leaders appointed a ten person steering committee, among whom were only three women. (Women continued, however, to engage in propaganda activities and sporadic rioting in their neighborhoods). The Allied Conference published a circular in both Yiddish and English, noting that "brave and honest men [were] now aiding the women" and declaring that the conference had "decided to help those butchers who [would] sell cheap kosher meat under the supervision of the rabbis and the conference." "The people feel very justly," continued the statement, "that they are being ground down, not only by the Beef Trust of the country, but also by the Jewish Beef Trust of the City."

On May 22, the Retail Butchers Association succumbed and affiliated itself with the boycott against the Trust. On May 27, Orthodox leaders, who had hesitated to express formal endorsement of the boycott, joined the fray. By June 5 the strike was concluded. The wholesale price of kosher meat was rolled back to nine cents a pound so that the retail price would be pegged at fourteen cents a pound. Kosher meal cooperatives, which were established during the strike in both Brooklyn and Harlem, continued in existence. While meat prices began to rise inexorably again in the period following the conclusion of the boycott, the movement can still be considered a qualified success.

The leaders of the boycott were not typical of other women political activists of the period. Unlike the majority of women organized in the nascent garment unions. they were not young. Unlike the female union leaders, they were housewives with children. The mean age of those boycott leaders who could be traced in the 1905 New York state manuscript census was 39. They ranged from Mamie Ghihnan, the thirty-two year old Russian-born wife of a tailor to Mrs. L. Finkelstein, a fifty-four year old member of the Women's Committee. All but two were more than thirty-five years of age at the time of the boycott. These women were mothers of large families, averaging 4.3 children apiece living at home. Fannie Levy, who initiated the call for the strike, was the mother of six children, all below the age of thirteen. None had fewer than three children. While only two women were United States citizens, the strike leaders were not, for the most part, recent arrivals to America. They had been living in New York City from three to twenty-seven years, with a median residence of eleven years. Having had sufficient lime to accommodate themselves to the American scene, they were not simply expressing traditional forms of cultural resistance to industrial society imported from the Old Country.

In socioeconomic terms, the women initiators of the boycott appear representative of the larger immigrant Jewish community of the Lower East Side. Their husbands were, by and large, employed as artisans in the garment industry, though three were self-employed small businessmen. The husband of Annie Block, a member of the Women's Committee, was a tailor, as were three other husbands. Fannie Levy's husband was a cloak maker and Bessie Norkin's a carpenter, while J. Jaffe's husband, Meyer, and Annie Levine's husband, Morris, topped the occupational scale as a real estate agent and storekeeper respectively. With one exception, all of their children above the age of sixteen were working—two-thirds of them in artisan trades and the remainder as clerks or low level business employees (e.g. salesladies). Only the eighteen year old son of the real estate agent was still in school (though his older brothers were employed as garment industry operators). Thus, the women formed not an elite in their community, but a true grass roots leadership.

It is clear from their statements and their activity that the women who led the boycott had a distinct economic objective in mind and a clear political strategy for achieving their goal. Unlike traditional food rioters, the Lower East Side housewives were not demanding the imposition of a just and popular price on retailers. Nor were they forcibly appropriating meat for purchase at a popularly determined fair price, though they did retain a traditional sense of a moral economy in which food should be available at prices which the working classes could afford. Rather, recognizing that prices were set by the operation of the laws of supply and demand, as modified, in this case, by the concentration of the wholesale meat industry, they hit upon a boycott of meat as the most effective way to dramatically curtail demand. They referred to themselves as strikers; those who did not comply with the boycott were called "scabs." When they were harassed in the Street by police, they complained that denial by police of their right to assemble was an attack on their freedom of speech. Thus, Lower East Side women were familiar with the political rhetoric of their day, with the workings of the market economy, and with the potential of consumers to affect the market.

While the impulse for the boycott originated in spontaneous outrage of women consumers at the price of kosher meat and their sense that they had been manipulated (or swindled, as they put it) by the retail butchers, who had sold out their customers in their agreement with the wholesalers, this incident was not simply an explosion of rage. It was a sustained, though limited, movement, whose success lay in its careful organization. As the *New York Herald* rightly commented, "These women were in earnest. For days they had been considering the situation, and when they decided on action, they perfected an organization, elected officers, . . . and even went so far as to take coins from their slender purses until there was an expense fund of eighty dollars with which to carry on the fight."

In fact, the neighborhood focus of the boycott organization proved to be its source of strength. The initial boycott committee, composed of nineteen women, numbered nine neighbors from Monroe Street, four from Cherry Street, and six from adjacent blocks. This was not the anonymous city so often portrayed by antiurban polemicists and historians but a neighborhood community whose residents maintained close ties. The first show of strength on May 15th was preceded by an early morning house-to-house canvas of housewives in the heart of the boycott area. A similar canvas occurred the next day in Harlem under the aegis of local women. Rooted in the neighborhood, where many activities were quasi-public rather than strictly private, housewives were able to exert moral (as well as physical) suasion upon the women whom they saw on a daily basis. They assumed the existence of collective goals and the right to demand shared sacrifices. Individual desires for the consumption of meat were to be subordinated to the larger public good. As one boycott enthusiast stated while grabbing meat from a girl leaving a butcher store, "If we can't eat meat, the customers can't eat meat." Shouting similar sentiments in another incident, striking women attempted to remove the meat from cholent pots which their neighbors had brought to a local bakery on a Friday afternoon. Participants in the boycott picketed local butchers and also resolved not to speak to the "scabs" in their midst. The constant presence in the neighborhood of the housewife leaders of the boycott made it difficult for individuals to evade their surveillance. The neighborhood, a

form of female network, thus provided the locus of community for the boycott: all were giving up meat together, celebrating dairy shabbosim together, and contributing together to the boycott fund.

The women who organized and led the boycott considered themselves the natural leaders of such an enterprise. As consumers and housewives, they saw their task as complementary to that of their wage-earning spouses: "Our husbands work hard," stated one of the leaders at the initial planning meeting. "They try their best to bring a few cents into the house. We must manage to spend as little as possible. We will not give away our last few cents to the butcher and let our children go barefoot.' In response, the women shouted, "We will not be silent; we will overturn the world." Describing themselves as soldiers, they determined to circulate leaflets calling upon all women to "join the great women's war." An appeal to their "worthy sisters," published by the Ladies' Anti-Beef Trust in the *Forward*, expressed similar sentiments, calling for "help . . . in the name of humanity in this great struggle which we have undertaken out of need."

Sharper formulations of class resentment mingled with pride in their own talents in some of the women's shouts in the street demonstrations. One woman was heard lamenting to another, "Your children must go to work, and the millionaires snatch the last bit from our mouths." Another called out, "My husband brings me eight dollars a week. Should I give it away to the butcher? What would the landlord say?" Still another screamed, "They think women aren't people, that they can bluff us; we'll show them that we are more people than the fat millionaires who suck our blood." When the son of the Chief Rabbi, who supervised the kashrut of the meat, passed through, the area, he was met with shouts of "Trust—Kosher *Korobke*," a reference to the kosher meat tax, much despised by the poor in Czarist Russia.

The ringleaders who were arrested and charged with disorderly conduct defined their behavior in political terms and considered it both just and appropriate to their status as housewives. "Did you throw meat on the street?" Rosa Peskin was asked. "Certainly," she replied. "I should have looked it in the teeth?" When the judge condescendingly commented, "What do you know of a trust? It's no business of yours," she responded, "Whose business is it, then, that our pockets are empty . . . ?" "What do you have against a woman who has bought meat," the judge persisted. "I have nothing against her," retorted Peskin. "It doesn't matter to me what others want to do. But it's because of others that we must suffer." Rebecca Ablowitz also presented the boycotters' rationale to the judge: "We're not rioting. Only see how thin our children are, our husbands have no more strength to work harder . . . if we stay home and cry, what good will that do us?"

DRAWING CONCLUSIONS:

1. What were the underlying causes of the Kosher Meat Boycott of 1902?
2. What can we learn from the case of the meat boycott about the causes of the social divisions of the age of industrialization?

ECONOMIC DATA

Prior to the twentieth century, the United States government did not collect comprehensive economic data. Late nineteenth-century economic statistics are thus estimates based on the efforts of economic historians to reconstruct standard economic data from available sources. Nonetheless, such estimates can be quite useful when considering the causes of the social and political upheavals of the period.

GUIDING QUESTIONS:

1. What do these statistics indicate about the social and economic changes experienced by Americans in the late 1800s?
2. What do these statistics indicate about the actual economic conditions experienced by Americans and particularly by wage workers and farmers?
3. How do people's perceptions, as expressed in the various primary source documents provided, compare with actual economic statistics?

PER CAPITA GROSS DOMESTIC PRODUCT (GDP)

Gross Domestic Product (GDP) is the standard measure of the total value of goods and services produced by a national economy. Per capita GDP measures the value of all goods and services produced divided by the nation's population. Per capita GDP thus measures the value of goods and services produced per person within the national economy. The statistics provided are adjusted to take into account the changing value of the dollar.

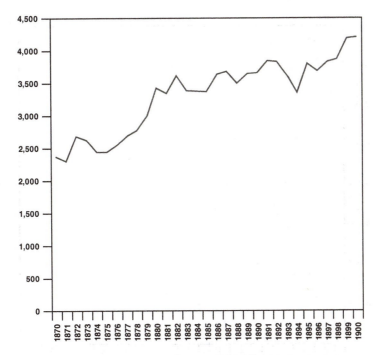

FIGURE 3. REAL GDP PER CAPITA, 1870–1900 (1996 DOLLARS).
Source: *Historical Statistics of the United States: Earliest Times to the Present*, Millennial Edition, Vol. 3 (Cambridge University Press, 2006), 3-25, 3-26.

INDUSTRIAL PRODUCTION

The Index of Industrial Production measures the real value (adjusted for the changing value of the dollar) of the nation's manufacturing, mining, and utilities industries. Since utility production (such as electrical generation) was a small portion of the national economy in the late nineteenth century, the statistics provided include only manufacturing and mining.

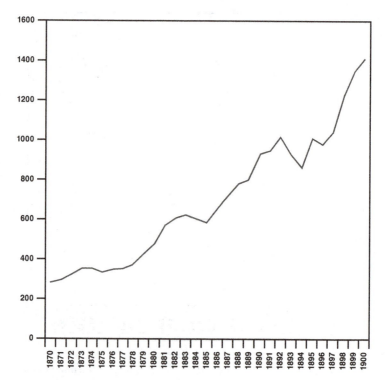

FIGURE 4. INDEX OF INDUSTRIAL PRODUCTION, 1870–1900 (1849–50 = 100).
Source: *Historical Statistics of the United States: Earliest Times to the Present,* Millennial Edition, Vol. 3 (Cambridge University Press, 2006), 3-25, 3-26.

CHANGING COMPOSITION OF THE WORKFORCE

These graphs demonstrate the growing percentage of the workforce engaged in non-agricultural pursuits. Note that both the agricultural and non-agricultural workforce were growing, as the nation's population expanded. The non-agricultural workforce, however, was growing much more rapidly.

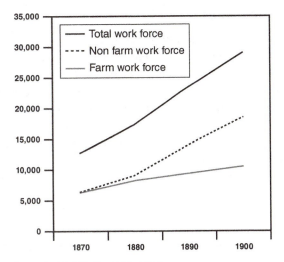

FIGURE 5. WORK FORCE (IN THOUSANDS), 1870–1900.
Source: *Historical Statistics of the United States: Earliest Times to the Present*, Millennial Edition, Vol. 2 (Cambridge University Press, 2006), 2-110.

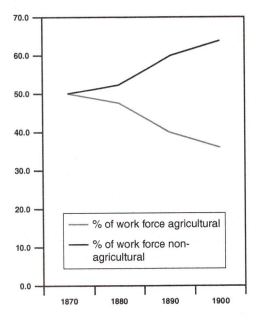

FIGURE 6. AGRICULTURAL AND NON-AGRICULTURAL PERCENTAGE OF WORK FORCE, 1870–1900.
Source: *Historical Statistics of the United States: Earliest Times to the Present*, Millennial Edition, Vol. 2 (Cambridge University Press, 2006), 2-110.

WAGES FOR UNSKILLED LABOR

This graph provides data on the hourly wages received by unskilled workers. It includes both an index of the actual money wages received and an index of money wages received adjusted for the changing value of the dollar. Note that since consumer prices were generally falling in the late nineteenth-century, the purchasing power of a dollar in wages increased over time. Also, keep in mind that this data only tells you how much an employed worker received for each hour he or she worked—it does not tell you how much individuals earned per week or per year. Levels of unemployment and underemployment (workers who want full-time work and can only find part-time work) also had a great influence on weekly and annual earnings, with unemployment and underemployment increasing significantly during economic downturns.

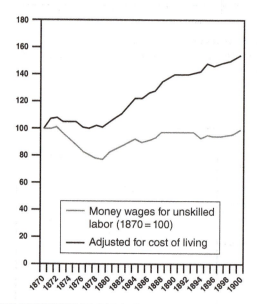

FIGURE 7. WAGES RECEIVED BY UNSKILLED LABORERS, 1870–1900.
Wage data: *Historical Statistics of the United States: Earliest Times to the Present*, Millennial Edition, Vol. 2 (Cambridge University Press, 2006), 2-256, 2-257.
Inflation data: David-Solar-based Consumer Price Index, *Historical Statistics of the United States: Earliest Times to the Present*, Millennial Edition, Vol. 2 (Cambridge University Press, 2006), 3-158.

UNEMPLOYMENT

There are no reliable unemployment statistics prior to 1890. We do, however, have data that documents the growth in unemployment during the harsh economic depression of the mid 1890s. This graph shows the percentage of the private (i.e., non-government) non-agricultural workforce that was unemployed for each year of the 1890s. For purposes of comparison, the unemployment rate in the United States since 1945 has varied between roughly 4% and 11% and only surpassed 10% twice during that period (during the recessions of 1981–1982 and 2008–2009).

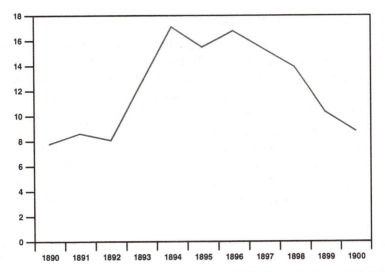

FIGURE 8. UNEMPLOYMENT – PERCENTAGE OF CIVILIAN PRIVATE NONFARM LABOR FORCE.
Source: *Historical Statistics of the United States: Earliest Times to the Present*, Millennial Edition, Vol. 2 (Cambridge University Press, 2006), 2-82.

CONCENTRATION OF WEALTH

There are no reliable national statistics on the distribution of wealth and income prior to 1900. Richard H. Steckel and Carolyn M. Moehling, however, have estimated the concentration of wealth for the state of Massachusetts dating back to 1820. Massachusetts was among the first states to undergo industrialization. The statistics for Massachusetts thus provide some insight into the impact of industrialization on wealth concentration. This table shows the percentage of all taxable wealth in the state that was held by the wealthiest 20%, 5%, and 1% of households. Due to limitations in the sources, the data is limited to male-headed households. (The vast majority of households at the time were headed by males.)

Share of Taxable Wealth of Male Household Heads Held by

Year	Top 20%	Top 5%	Top 1%
1820	72.0	40.5	20.3
1830	77.6	49.2	28.9
1840	78.3	45.0	20.0
1850	85.8	55.7	33.4
1860	88.1	55.7	27.0
1870	90.1	56.7	27.2
1880	93.7	60.3	29 1
1890	Not Available	Not Available	Not Available
1900	97.3	70.5	37.2

FIGURE 9. DISTRIBUTION OF WEALTH IN MASSACHUSETTS, 1820–1900
Source: *Historical Statistics of the United States: Earliest Times to the Present*, Millennial Edition, Vol. 2 (Cambridge University Press, 2006), 2-659.

WHEAT, COTTON, AND CORN PRICES

These graphs present the prices of three major agricultural commodities in the late nineteenth century. Wheat was the main product produced by farmers in Great Plains states like Kansas, Nebraska, and the Dakotas. Corn was more common in prairie states like Iowa and Illinois. In southern states such as Georgia, Alabama, and Mississippi, the main product was cotton. The Farmers' Alliance and People's Party drew much greater support from cotton and wheat producing states than corn producing states. The prices in the figures reflect those within national markets. The actual prices received by farmers would have been somewhat less. These statistics, though, are important as an indication of price trends over time. The prices paid by farmers for supplies also fell during this period. The main impact of falling prices was that it made it more difficult for farmers to pay off their debts.

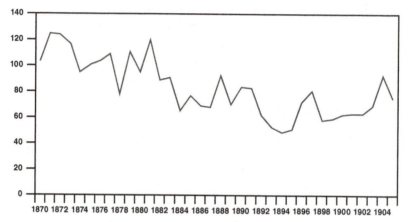

FIGURE 10. PRICE OF WHEAT, 1870–1905: CENTS PER BUSHEL.
Source: *Historical Statistics of the United States: Earliest Times to the Present*, Millennial Edition, Vol. 4 (Cambridge University Press, 2006), 4-102.

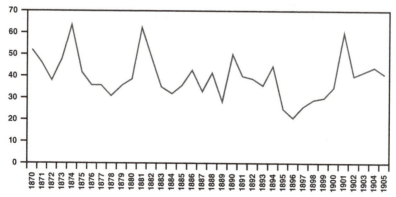

FIGURE 11. PRICE OF CORN, 1870–1905: CENTS PER BUSHEL.
Source: *Historical Statistics of the United States: Earliest Times to the Present*, Millennial Edition, Vol. 4 (Cambridge University Press, 2006), 4-97, 4-98.

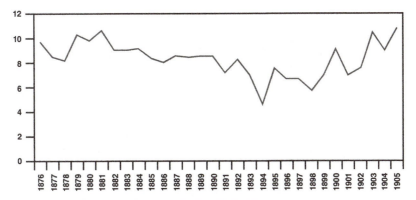

FIGURE 12. PRICE OF COTTON, 1876–1905: CENTS PER POUND.

Note: Exact prices prior to 1876 are not available. The early to mid 1870s, however, were generally a period of falling cotton prices.

Source: *Historical Statistics of the United States: Earliest Times to the Present*, Millennial Edition, Vol. 4 (Cambridge University Press, 2006), 4-111.

DRAWING CONCLUSIONS:

1. What do these statistics contribute to our understanding of the social and political conflicts of the age of industrialization?
2. If a Populist had access to these statistics, what conclusions do you think he would have drawn? Samuel Gompers? Andrew Carnegie?

ADDITIONAL RESOURCES

Dubofsky, Melvyn. *Industrialism and the American Worker, 1865–1920*, 3rd ed. Wheeling, IL: Harlan Davidson, 1996.

Ewen, Elizabeth. *Immigrant Women in the Land of Dollars: Life and Culture on the Lower East Side, 1890–1925*. New York: Monthly Review Press, 1985.

Goodwyn, Lawrence. *Democratic Promise: The Populist Moment in America*. New York: Oxford University Press, 1976.

Hicks, John Donald. *The Populist Revolt: A History of the Farmers' Alliance and People's Party*. Minneapolis: University of Minnesota Press, 1931.

Gutman, Herbert G. *Work, Culture, and Society: Essays in American Working-Class and Social History*. New York: Vintage Books, 1976.

Hofstadter, Richard. *The Age of Reform: From Bryan to F.D.R.* New York: Knopf, 1955.

Krause, Paul. *The Battle for Homestead, 1880–1892: Politics, Culture, and Steel*. Pittsburgh, PA: University of Pittsburgh Press, 1992.

Livesay, Harold C. *Andrew Carnegie and the Rise of Big Business*. Boston: Little, Brown, 1975.

Montgomery, David. *The Fall of the House of Labor: The Workplace, the State, and American Labor Activism, 1865–1920*. New York: Cambridge University Press, 1987.

Postel, Charles. *The Populist Vision*. New York: Oxford University Press, 2007.

Trachtenberg, Alan. *The Incorporation of America: Culture and Society in the Gilded Age*. New York: Hill and Wang, 1982.

INDEX

Note: In this index, page numbers in *italics* refer to figures and *t* refers to pages with tables.